THE ASTROLOGER'S BOOK OF CHARTS

A COLLECTION OF HOROSCOPES
BY FRANK C. CLIFFORD

FLARE PUBLICATIONS
THE LONDON SCHOOL OF ASTROLOGY

First published in 2009 by Flare Publications
in conjunction with the London School of Astrology
BCM Planets, London WC1N 3XX, England, UK
Tel: 0700 2 33 44 55
www.flareuk.com and www.londonschoolofastrology.co.uk
email: admin@londonschoolofastrology.co.uk

A CIP catalogue record for this book is available from the British Library

ISBN: 978-1-903353-08-0

To contact the author, please email him at info@flareuk.com
www.flareuk.com

Astrological charts by Io Edition, Time Cycles Research
Cover: Catherine Keane
Layout: Craig Knottenbelt

Data Editing: Sy Scholfield
Text Editing: Jane Struthers

Thank Yous

This book has benefited greatly from the care, precision and expertise of my friends Jane Struthers and Sy Scholfield. Sy, who has become one of the great data collectors, checked every piece of information and provided many birth names, coordinates and additional details. I would also like to thank Cat Keane for the cover artwork and Craig Knottenbelt for help with InDesign.

I'd like to dedicate this book to Kai
and to all the astrologers who share my passion for accurate data when teaching astrology
and to past, current and future students of the London School of Astrology

I am also proud that this book will be a reference book not only for the LSA
but for the Mayo School of Astrology, run by my pal Wendy Stacey.

Introduction

In 2003, when I was in the process of finishing the revision of *British Entertainers: the Astrological Profiles*, I was honoured that my friend, the astrologer and data collector Lois Rodden, agreed to write the foreword to the book. At the time she was terminally ill, and sadly she died before the book was published. In the foreword, Lois said, 'The most valuable books in our library are our reference books. Among them, data collections stand out as the basic tool in our study of astrology. Without them our study is entirely theoretical. Moreover, when we look at the charts of family and friends, we need examples of Mars in the 1st House or Jupiter conjunct the MC to see how this has worked out in the lives of other people. As devoted as we are in our study of astrology, without horoscopes to examine, we cannot see how the planets work in real lives.' This is one of the reasons I put this book together and, no doubt, one of the reasons you have it in your hands.

As I was preparing to begin another academic year of teaching at the London School of Astrology, I had the idea to create a data book for my students (and astrology teachers) in order to give them a number of new, well-known and hard-to-find horoscopes as examples in classes and for their own research.

From my data and birth record files and reference books, I've compiled the birth data and horoscopes of 150 individuals: entertainers and artists, entrepreneurs, politicians and activists, sportspeople, royalty, writers, pioneers and philosophers, lawbreakers and other notable people whose lives and horoscopes make for interesting study and research. I've hand-picked the charts that I hope will be of interest – so inside, there's not only the history-makers and the record-breakers, but also other people who have lived fascinating, eventful lives. The data on which the charts are calculated are based on the most accurate, sourced information available at the time of going to press. Any updates will be printed in future editions and listed online at www.flareuk. com (Do please get in touch if you have updates or queries.)

We enhance our understanding of astrology by reading biographies and listening to life stories of friends and family. What has always kept my interest in astrology is the excitement of discovering someone's birth data, calculating the chart and then looking at how their lives reflect and 'speak' their charts. But sometimes there's a temptation to look at the chart and then apply what we know about planets, signs and houses to people, simply based on their chart patterns. The student and working astrologer, I believe, will always benefit from reversing this process: if we research themes, traits and experiences common to people and *then* look for common factors in their horoscopes that link these, we build up our own understanding of planetary principles at work. We can gather a rich and diverse arsenal of traits and experiences from our own observations. This way, we can avoid reinforcing stereotypes or sticking to outdated interpretations. Every chart teaches us something new because every person has their own way of playing out their horoscope: each has a unique set of stories, experiences and viewpoints. Each planet, sign and house has a wide spectrum of meaning and dominion that fall under that particular 'type'.

This volume can be used alongside my book *The Heart of the Chart: Playing Astrological Detective* (2009), which outlines my own method of delineating any horoscope. I do hope you enjoy studying the horoscopes within – and have fun researching the profiles, too.

Frank Clifford, April 2009

The Layout

On each of the pages, you'll find the following:

Name – an alphabetical listing of the individual

A brief biography – often with some key dates

A worksheet – space to note down and analyse key factors in the horoscope (from the elemental and modal balance to the major themes and aspect configurations)

Two horoscope wheels – the top chart is calculated using Equal houses and the bottom chart using Placidean. Unfortunately, due to the chart style used, there are no house numbers nor is there a listing of Chiron. There is space on the worksheet to list Chiron and other bodies under the heading 'Other chart points'.

Birth data and source – the birth date, time, time signature (including a +/- calculation to GMT), place and coordinates (often very precise). The source(s) of the data is listed. Where I have a copy on file, this has been noted too. Occasionally, I have listed the birth data of a key person in the individual's life.

Name at birth – where I have the birth certificate or note on file, or where a birth record is available to check online or in person, I have been able to confirm the birth name; otherwise I have relied on other sources online or from astrologers who have seen these documents. There is often debate around birth names, but I have attempted to list the names given at birth rather than any given at baptism or names adopted at a later date.

Much of the data have come from my own files (some have never been published before), my Solar Fire compendium, the Astrodatabank program, Scotland's People website, directly from a number of data collectors including Caroline Gerard and Sy Scholfield, and from the collections *Contemporary American Horoscopes* by Janice Mackay-Saunders (Astrolabe disk, 1990) and *The Gauquelin Book of American Charts* by Michel and Françoise Gauquelin (ACS 1982). I have not repeated data from my *British Entertainers* book.

RR and data collectors – I have chosen charts where there is documented evidence to vouch for their accuracy. For professional standards, it is vital that data presented to the astrological community be as accurate and fully sourced as possible. Be suspicious of any data from internet sites or publications that do not document their data sources. It is recommended that all data are classified using the simple Rodden Rating (RR) system:

AA – Data from birth certificate, hospital or governmental birth record, notes from the Vital Statistics/Registries, notations in a family Bible, baby book or family written record. Although birth times may be rounded off or, on occasion, information may be in error, this is the best evidence of data accuracy available.

A – Data from the person, family member, friend or associate. Also included are newspaper birth announcements, as well as birth times given within a 'window of time' of thirty minutes (e.g. 'between 3.30pm and 4.00pm').

B – Data from biographies, autobiographies and personal websites, where no other source is given.

C – Caution, data not validated. No source; vague, rectified/speculative data, 'personal' ambiguous sources, approximate birth times (e.g. 'early morning', 'around lunchtime').

DD – Dirty Data. Two or more unsubstantiated quotes of time, place or date. Any unverified data that are contradicted by another source.

I have attempted to give full credit to the astrologers who have collected the data.

The Profiles (by Sun, Moon and Ascendant sign)

SUN IN ARIES
- Maya Angelou ☽♎ A♌
- Pope Benedict XVI ☽♎ A♓
- Joseph Campbell ☽♌ A♎
- Aretha Franklin ☽♋ A♏
- Linda Goodman ☽♎ A♈
- Billie Holiday ☽♑ A♒
- Erica Jong ☽♋ A♊
- Diana Ross ☽♉ A♏
- Tennessee Williams ☽♒ A♑

SUN IN TAURUS
- David Beckham ☽♑ A♉
- Tony Blair ☽♒ A♊
- Cher ☽♑ A♋
- Salvador Dalï ☽♈ A♋
- Queen Elizabeth II ☽♌ A♑
- Sigmund Freud ☽♊ A♏
- Adolf Hitler ☽♑ A♎
- Jim Jones ☽♈ A♑
- Liberace ☽♐ A♑
- George Lucas ☽♒ A♉
- Karl Marx ☽♉ A♒
- Michael Moore ☽♑ A♌
- Bertrand Russell ☽♎ A♏
- Aaron Spelling ☽♋ A♌
- Barbra Streisand ☽♌ A♈
- Orson Welles ☽♒ A♊

SUN IN GEMINI
- Johnny Depp ☽♑ A♌
- Arthur Conan Doyle ☽♒ A♊
- Bob Dylan ☽♉ A♐
- Anne Frank ☽♌ A♌
- Judy Garland ☽♐ A♋
- Steffi Graf ☽♊ A♊
- Thomas Hardy ☽♋ A♌
- Angelina Jolie ☽♈ A♋
- John F. Kennedy ☽♍ A♎
- Marilyn Monroe ☽♒ A♌
- Salman Rushdie ☽♊ A♉
- Marquis de Sade ☽♍ A♏
- Peter Sutcliffe ☽♋ A♐
- Donald Trump ☽♐ A♌
- Queen Victoria ☽♊ A♊
- Dr Ruth Westheimer ☽♐ A♊
- Venus Williams ☽♌ A♎

SUN IN CANCER
- Pamela Anderson ☽♈ A♊
- Richard Branson ☽♍ A♌
- George W. Bush ☽♎ A♌
- Barbara Cartland ☽♈ A♈
- Princess Diana ☽♒ A♐
- Harrison Ford ☽♋ A♎
- Leona Helmsley ☽♒ A♋
- Myra Hindley ☽♏ A♊
- Carl Lewis ☽♒ A♌
- Emmeline Pankhurst ☽♍ A♒
- Camilla Parker Bowles ☽♋ A♌
- Nancy Reagan ☽♌ A♎
- O.J. Simpson ☽♓ A♌
- Sylvester Stallone ☽♎ A♐

SUN IN LEO
- Coco Chanel ☽♓ A♐
- Bill Clinton ☽♉ A♎
- Amelia Earhart ☽♊ A♉
- Roger Federer ☽♏ A♍
- George Galloway ☽♓ A♌
- Alex Haley ☽♏ A♌
- Whitney Houston ☽♈ A♓
- Carl Gustav Jung ☽♉ A♒
- Jacqueline Kennedy ☽♈ A♏
- Monica Lewinsky ☽♉ A♎
- Madonna ☽♍ A♍
- Mata Hari ☽♓ A♏
- Benito Mussolini ☽♊ A♏
- Barack Obama ☽♊ A♒
- JonBenét Ramsey ☽♒ A♊
- Gene Roddenberry ☽♓ A♋
- Arnold Schwarzenegger ☽♑ A♋
- George Bernard Shaw ☽♉ A♊
- Percy Bysshe Shelley ☽♓ A♉
- Martha Stewart ☽♐ A♏

SUN IN VIRGO
- Cherie Blair ☽♌ A♌
- Queen Elizabeth I ☽♉ A♑
- Greta Garbo ☽♉ A♊
- D.H. Lawrence ☽♎ A♏
- Mary Shelley ☽♐ A♋
- Neale Donald Walsch ☽♑ A♌
- H.G. Wells ☽♒ A♒
- Amy Winehouse ☽♑ A♊

SUN IN LIBRA
- Brigitte Bardot ☽♊ A♐
- Deepak Chopra ☽♍ A♓
- F. Scott Fitzgerald ☽♉ A♒
- Marion Jones ☽♑ A♏
- Gillian McKeith ☽♍ A♊
- Martina Navratilova ☽♈ A♈
- Lee Harvey Oswald ☽♑ A♋
- Anita Roddick ☽♈ A♐
- Eleanor Roosevelt ☽♋ A♐
- Marie Stopes ☽♓ A♍
- Margaret Thatcher ☽♌ A♏
- Oscar Wilde ☽♌ A♍

SUN IN SCORPIO
- Prince Charles ☽♉ A♌
- Leonardo DiCaprio ☽♎ A♎
- George Eliot ☽♑ A♏
- Jodie Foster ☽♍ A♐
- Princess Grace ☽♓ A♏
- Kray Twins ☽♑ A♋
- Charles Manson ☽♒ A♉
- Pablo Picasso ☽♐ A♌
- Sylvia Plath ☽♎ A♒
- Don Simpson ☽♏ A♐
- Robert Louis Stevenson ☽♓ A♒
- Ted Turner ☽♎ A♐

SUN IN SAGITTARIUS
- Woody Allen ☽♒ A♍
- Jane Austen ☽♎ A♍
- Winston Churchill ☽♌ A♍
- Walt Disney ☽♎ A♍
- Jane Fonda ☽♌ A♑
- Florence Griffith-Joyner ☽♍ A♎
- Jimi Hendrix ☽♋ A♐
- Bruce Lee ☽♏ A♐
- Jim Morrison ☽♉ A♒
- Dennis Nilsen ☽♋ A♎
- Brad Pitt ☽♑ A♐
- Frank Sinatra ☽♓ A♎
- Britney Spears ☽♒ A♎
- Steven Spielberg ☽♏ A♋
- Tina Turner ☽♊ A♌
- Dionne Warwick ☽♉ A♉

SUN IN CAPRICORN
- Muhammad Ali ☽♒ A♌
- Ian Brady ☽♑ A♉
- John DeLorean ☽♊ A♈
- Marlene Dietrich ☽♌ A♍
- Heidi Fleiss ☽♈ A♒
- Janis Joplin ☽♋ A♒
- Martin Luther King, Jr ☽♓ A♉
- Marilyn Manson ☽♌ A♌
- Richard Nixon ☽♒ A♍
- Dolly Parton ☽♍ A♍
- Elvis Presley ☽♓ A♐
- Tiger Woods ☽♐ A♍

SUN IN AQUARIUS
- Farrah Fawcett ☽♋ A♋
- Germaine Greer ☽♉ A♒
- John McEnroe ☽♊ A♎
- Wolfgang A. Mozart ☽♐ A♍
- Justin Timberlake ☽♐ A♌
- John Travolta ☽♍ A♋

SUN IN PISCES
- Gordon Brown ☽♌ A♈
- Karen Carpenter ☽♌ A♋
- Kurt Cobain ☽♋ A♍
- Albert Einstein ☽♐ A♋
- Christine Keeler ☽♉ A♊
- Anaïs Nin ☽♑ A♎
- Anthony Robbins ☽♈ A♎
- Betty Shine ☽♒ A♉

MUHAMMAD ALI

Sporting legend; three-time World Heavyweight boxing
champion; took a stand against racism and war in the USA

Sun ....

Moon ....

Ascendant ....

      Chart Ruler ....

Fire ....

Earth ....

Air ....

Water ....

Cardinal ....

Fixed ....

Mutable ....

Mutual Reception: Sign emphasis:

Unaspected: House emphasis:

Retrograde: Singletons/Duets:

Other chart points:

Equal Houses

Placidus Houses

ASPECTS & CONFIGURATIONS

THEMES & OTHER OBSERVATIONS

Born 17 January 1942, 18:35 CST (+6)
Louisville, Kentucky, USA (38n15, 85w46)

Source: Birth certificate, copy on file.

RR: AA   (Cassius Marcellus Clay, Jr)
    Data Collectors: Edwin Steinbrecher; M. and F. Gauquelin

Notes:

WOODY ALLEN

Film auteur, director, writer, actor, comedian, jazz
clarinetist; neurotic, self-doubting, analytical persona

Sun ....

Moon ....

Ascendant ....

     Chart Ruler ....

Fire ....

Earth ....

Air ....

Water ....

Cardinal ....

Fixed ....

Mutable ....

Mutual Reception: Sign emphasis:

Unaspected: House emphasis:

Retrograde: Singletons/Duets:

Other chart points:

ASPECTS & CONFIGURATIONS

THEMES & OTHER OBSERVATIONS

Equal Houses

Placidus Houses

Born 1 December 1935, 22:55 EST (+5)
Bronx, New York, USA (40n51, 73w54)

Source: Birth certificate, copy on file.

RR: AA

(Allan Stewart Konigsberg)
Data Collector: Lois Rodden

Notes:

PAMELA ANDERSON

Sex symbol, *Playboy* model, actress (TV's *Baywatch*), animal
rights activist; highly-publicized, tumultuous romantic life

Sun ....

Moon ....

Ascendant ....

      Chart Ruler ....

Fire ....

Earth ....

Air ....

Water ....

Cardinal ....

Fixed ....

Mutable ....

Mutual Reception: Sign emphasis:

Unaspected: House emphasis:

Retrograde: Singletons/Duets:

Other chart points:

Equal Houses

Placidus Houses

ASPECTS & CONFIGURATIONS

THEMES & OTHER OBSERVATIONS

Born 1 July 1967, 04:08 PDT (+7)
Ladysmith, Canada (48n58, 123w49)

Source: 'The Sunday Telegraph' quotes her birth announcement
in 'The Ladysmith-Chemainus Chronicle', copy on file.

RR: A

(Pamela Denise Anderson)
Data Collector: Nicholas Campion

Notes:

MAYA ANGELOU

Honoured poet and writer of six autobiographical volumes
celebrating the human spirit, courage and renewed hope

Sun ....

Moon ....

Ascendant ....

      Chart Ruler ....

Fire ....

Earth ....

Air ....

Water ....

Cardinal ....

Fixed ....

Mutable ....

Mutual Reception: Sign emphasis:

Unaspected: House emphasis:

Retrograde: Singletons/Duets:

Other chart points:

Equal Houses

Placidus Houses

ASPECTS & CONFIGURATIONS

THEMES & OTHER OBSERVATIONS

Born 4 April 1928, 14:10 CST (+6)
St Louis, Missouri, USA (38n38, 90w12)

Source: Birth certificate quoted in 'Contemporary American
Horoscopes'.

RR: AA

(Marguerite Ann Johnson)
Data Collector: Janice Mackay-Saunders

Notes:

JANE AUSTEN

Novelist whose witty volumes satirized novels of sensibility,
often with a biting, ironic social commentary

Sun ....

Moon ....

Ascendant ....

      Chart Ruler ....

Fire ....

Earth ....

Air ....

Water ....

Cardinal ....

Fixed ....

Mutable ....

Mutual Reception: Sign emphasis:

Unaspected: House emphasis:

Retrograde: Singletons/Duets:

Other chart points:

Equal Houses

Placidus Houses

ASPECTS & CONFIGURATIONS

THEMES & OTHER OBSERVATIONS

Born 16 December 1775, 23:30 LAT (+0:01:11)
Steventon, England (51n14, 1w13)

Source: Father's letter states 'before midnight', quoted in
Isabelle Pagan's 'From Pioneer to Poet'.

RR: A

(Jane Austen)
Data Collector: Isabelle Pagan

Notes:

BRIGITTE BARDOT

Actress-model; international sensation as a sensual risqué
'sex kitten'; controversial animal and human rights activist

Sun ....

Moon ....

Ascendant ....

      Chart Ruler ....

Fire ....

Earth ....

Air ....

Water ....

Cardinal ....

Fixed ....

Mutable ....

Mutual Reception: Sign emphasis:

Unaspected: House emphasis:

Retrograde: Singletons/Duets:

Other chart points:

Equal Houses

Placidus Houses

ASPECTS & CONFIGURATIONS

THEMES & OTHER OBSERVATIONS

Born 28 September 1934, 13:15 GDT (-1)
Paris, France (48n52, 2e20)

Source: Birth certificate.

RR: AA

(Brigitte Anne-Marie Bardot)
Data Collectors: M. and F. Gauquelin

Notes:

DAVID BECKHAM

Footballer, photogenic fashion icon, and multi-media global
commercial brand with wife Victoria Adams (born 17/04/74)

Sun ....

Moon ....

Ascendant ....

　　　Chart Ruler ....

Fire ....

Earth ....

Air ....

Water ....

Cardinal ....

Fixed ....

Mutable ....

Mutual Reception:　　Sign emphasis:

Unaspected:　　　　　House emphasis:

Retrograde:　　　　　Singletons/Duets:

Other chart points:

Equal Houses

ASPECTS & CONFIGURATIONS

THEMES & OTHER OBSERVATIONS

Placidus Houses

Born 2 May 1975, 06:17 GDT (-1)
Whipps Cross Hospital, Leytonstone, London, England
(51n35, 0w00)

Source: Biography 'David Beckham My Son' by Ted Beckham,
p.10 (Boxtree, 2005). Birth certificate (without a birth
time) is printed on p.12.
RR: B　　　　　　　　　　　(David Robert Joseph Beckham)
　　　　　　　　Data Collectors: Frank Clifford; Sy Scholfield

Notes:

POPE BENEDICT XVI

Elected Pope on 19/4/2005; former university professor and
Archbishop; Roman Catholic theologian and author

Sun ....

Moon ....

Ascendant ....

    Chart Ruler ....

Fire ....

Earth ....

Air ....

Water ....

Cardinal ....

Fixed ....

Mutable ....

Mutual Reception: Sign emphasis:

Unaspected: House emphasis:

Retrograde: Singletons/Duets:

Other chart points:

Equal Houses

Placidus Houses

ASPECTS & CONFIGURATIONS

THEMES & OTHER OBSERVATIONS

Born 16 April 1927, 04:15 MET (−1)
Marktl, Germany (48n15, 12e51)

Source: Birth certificate.

RR: AA

(Joseph Alois Ratzinger)
Data Collectors: Hans Hinrich Taeger; Grazia Bordoni

Notes:

CHERIE BLAIR

Barrister (1976–) and QC (1995–), specializing in employment and discrimination law; married Tony Blair 29/3/1980

Sun ....

Moon ....

Ascendant ....

      Chart Ruler ....

Fire ....

Earth ....

Air ....

Water ....

Cardinal ....

Fixed ....

Mutable ....

Mutual Reception: Sign emphasis:

Unaspected: House emphasis:

Retrograde: Singletons/Duets:

Other chart points:

Equal Houses

Placidus Houses

ASPECTS & CONFIGURATIONS

THEMES & OTHER OBSERVATIONS

Born 23 September 1954, 01:20 GDT (-1)
Bury, Lancashire, England (53n36, 2w17)

Source: Her to Frank Clifford in 1996, quoting her father.
In 2000 her PA's letter to David Fisher gave 01:30. (Cherie
was baptised Theresa Cara Booth.)

RR: A   (Cherie Booth)
      Data Collectors: Frank Clifford; David Fisher

Notes:

TONY BLAIR

Labour Party leader (from 21/7/1994) and the UK's three-term elected Prime Minister (2/5/1997 to 27/6/2007)

Sun ....

Moon ....

Ascendant ....

     Chart Ruler ....

Fire ....

Earth ....

Air ....

Water ....

Cardinal ....

Fixed ....

Mutable ....

Mutual Reception: Sign emphasis:

Unaspected: House emphasis:

Retrograde: Singletons/Duets:

Other chart points:

Equal Houses

Placidus Houses

ASPECTS & CONFIGURATIONS

THEMES & OTHER OBSERVATIONS

Born 6 May 1953, 06:10 GDT (-1)
Edinburgh, Scotland (55n57, 3w13)

Source: Birth certificate.

RR: AA   (Anthony Charles Lynton Blair)
Data Collector: Caroline Gerard

Notes:

IAN BRADY

'Moors Murderer' with Myra Hindley (qv); found guilty on
6/5/1966; declared insane in 1995; hunger strike from 1999

Sun ....

Moon ....

Ascendant ....

     Chart Ruler ....

Fire ....

Earth ....

Air ....

Water ....

Cardinal ....

Fixed ....

Mutable ....

Mutual Reception: Sign emphasis:

Unaspected: House emphasis:

Retrograde: Singletons/Duets:

Other chart points:

Equal Houses

Placidus Houses

ASPECTS & CONFIGURATIONS

THEMES & OTHER OBSERVATIONS

Born 2 January 1938, 12:40 GMT (+0)
Glasgow, Scotland (55n53, 4w15)

Source: Birth certificate, copy on file.

RR: AA   (Ian Stewart)
                                    Data Collector: Victoria Shaw

Notes:

RICHARD BRANSON

Entrepreneur of the Virgin global media brand; attempted
several world record-breaking boat and balloon challenges

Sun ....

Moon ....

Ascendant ....

      Chart Ruler ....

Fire ....

Earth ....

Air ....

Water ....

Cardinal ....

Fixed ....

Mutable ....

Mutual Reception: Sign emphasis:

Unaspected: House emphasis:

Retrograde: Singletons/Duets:

Other chart points:

Equal Houses

Placidus Houses

ASPECTS & CONFIGURATIONS

THEMES & OTHER OBSERVATIONS

Born 18 July 1950, 07:00 GDT (-1)
Blackheath, England (51n28, 0w00)

Source: His PA Saskia Kitchen to Frank Clifford, quoting
Branson's mother.

RR: A   (Richard Charles Nicholas Branson)
Data Collector: Frank Clifford

Notes:

GORDON BROWN

MP from 9/6/1983; UK's Labour Party Chancellor from
2/5/1997 before becoming Prime Minister on 27/6/2007

Sun ....

Moon ....

Ascendant ....

      Chart Ruler ....

Fire ....

Earth ....

Air ....

Water ....

Cardinal ....

Fixed ....

Mutable ....

Mutual Reception: Sign emphasis:

Unaspected: House emphasis:

Retrograde: Singletons/Duets:

Other chart points:

Equal Houses

Placidus Houses

ASPECTS & CONFIGURATIONS

THEMES & OTHER OBSERVATIONS

Born 20 February 1951, 08:40 GMT (+0)
Giffnock, Scotland (55n48, 4w18)

Source: Birth certificate (confirmed by Caroline Gerard,
11/08).

RR: AA   (James Gordon Brown)
       Data Collector: Paul Wright; Caroline Gerard

Notes:

GEORGE W. BUSH

Governor of Texas from 22/1/1995; sworn in as US President
on 20/1/2001 after voting irregularities in 7/11/2000 election

Sun ....

Moon ....

Ascendant ....

      Chart Ruler ....

Fire ....

Earth ....

Air ....

Water ....

Cardinal ....

Fixed ....

Mutable ....

Mutual Reception: Sign emphasis:

Unaspected: House emphasis:

Retrograde: Singletons/Duets:

Other chart points:

Equal Houses

Placidus Houses

ASPECTS & CONFIGURATIONS

THEMES & OTHER OBSERVATIONS

Born 6 July 1946, 07:26 EDT (+4)
New Haven, Connecticut, USA (41n18, 72w56)

Source: Hospital records; same on birth certificate quoted in
'First Son: George W. Bush and the Bush Family Dynasty' by
Bill Minutaglio (Random House, 1999), p.24 and p.330.

RR: AA   (George Walker Bush)
                 Data Collectors: Kim Castilla; Wayne Turner

Notes:

JOSEPH CAMPBELL

Writer and professor on mythology, spirituality and the
journey of the hero; coined the phrase 'follow your bliss'

Sun ....

Moon ....

Ascendant ....

      Chart Ruler ....

Fire ....

Earth ....

Air ....

Water ....

Cardinal ....

Fixed ....

Mutable ....

Mutual Reception: Sign emphasis:

Unaspected: House emphasis:

Retrograde: Singletons/Duets:

Other chart points:

Equal Houses

Placidus Houses

ASPECTS & CONFIGURATIONS

THEMES & OTHER OBSERVATIONS

Born 26 March 1904, 19:25 EST (+5)
White Plains, New York, USA (41n02, 73w46)

Source: His mother to Erin Cameron in 1981. The exact birth
place is listed on his website.

RR: A

(Joseph John Campbell)
Data Collector: Erin Cameron

Notes:

KAREN CARPENTER

Singer and drummer; formed The Carpenters with brother
Richard; died after a lengthy battle with anorexia nervosa

Sun ....

Moon ....

Ascendant ....

    Chart Ruler ....

Fire ....

Earth ....

Air ....

Water ....

Cardinal ....

Fixed ....

Mutable ....

Mutual Reception: Sign emphasis:

Unaspected: House emphasis:

Retrograde: Singletons/Duets:

Other chart points:

Equal Houses

Placidus Houses

ASPECTS & CONFIGURATIONS

THEMES & OTHER OBSERVATIONS

Born 2 March 1950, 11:45 EST (+5)
New Haven, Connecticut, USA (41n18, 72w56)

Source: Note from birth registry. (Brother Richard Carpenter
was born 15 October 1946, 00:53 EST (+5), New Haven,
Connecticut, USA (41n18, 72w56). Same source.)

RR: AA   (Karen Anne Carpenter)
                  Data Collector: Edwin Steinbrecher

Notes:

BARBARA CARTLAND

Indefatigable, prolific romantic novelist (723 titles from 1923–2000); outspoken media personality; championed vitamin use

Sun ....

Moon ....

Ascendant ....

     Chart Ruler ....

Fire ....

Earth ....

Air ....

Water ....

Cardinal ....

Fixed ....

Mutable ....

Mutual Reception: Sign emphasis:

Unaspected: House emphasis:

Retrograde: Singletons/Duets:

Other chart points:

Equal Houses

Placidus Houses

ASPECTS & CONFIGURATIONS

THEMES & OTHER OBSERVATIONS

Born 9 July 1901, 23:40 GMT (+0)
Edgbaston, Birmingham, England (52n28, 1w57)

Source: Mother's diary quoted in a letter to Marc Penfield, copy in hand. Joan Revill quotes Cartland for 'shortly before midnight'; 23:45 given to Penny Thornton.

RR: AA   (Mary Barbara Hamilton Cartland)
    Data Collectors: Marc Penfield; Joan Revill; Penny Thornton

Notes:

COCO CHANEL

Fashion designer and businesswoman from 1909; noted for
her simple, classy and elegant *haute couture* creations

Sun ....

Moon ....

Ascendant ....

    Chart Ruler ....

Fire ....

Earth ....

Air ....

Water ....

Cardinal ....

Fixed ....

Mutable ....

Mutual Reception: Sign emphasis:

Unaspected: House emphasis:

Retrograde: Singletons/Duets:

Other chart points:

Equal Houses

Placidus Houses

ASPECTS & CONFIGURATIONS

THEMES & OTHER OBSERVATIONS

```
Born 19 August 1883, 16:00 LMT (+0:00:20)
Saumur, France (47n16, 0w05)

Source: Birth certificate printed in 'Chanel and Her World'
by Edmonde Charles-Roux, copy on file.


RR: AA                                    (Gabrielle Chanel)
                              Data Collector: Dana Holliday
```

Notes:

PRINCE CHARLES

Prince of Wales; married to Diana (qv) from 29/7/1981 to
26/8/1996; married Camilla Parker-Bowles (qv) on 9/4/2005

Sun ....

Moon ....

Ascendant ....

     Chart Ruler ....

Fire ....

Earth ....

Air ....

Water ....

Cardinal ....

Fixed ....

Mutable ....

Mutual Reception: Sign emphasis:

Unaspected: House emphasis:

Retrograde: Singletons/Duets:

Other chart points:

Equal Houses

Placidus Houses

ASPECTS & CONFIGURATIONS

THEMES & OTHER OBSERVATIONS

Born 14 November 1948, 21:14 GMT (+0)
Buckingham Palace, London, England (51n30, 0w08)

Source: Palace announcement quoted in newspapers on date,
copy on file.

RR: A   (Charles Philip Arthur George Windsor)
     Data Collector: Judith Gee

Notes:

CHER

Singer and actress (Oscar for *Moonstruck*, rel. 18/12/1987); met
co-star Sonny Bono in 11/1962, married until 27/6/1975

Sun ....

Moon ....

Ascendant ....

     Chart Ruler ....

Fire ....

Earth ....

Air ....

Water ....

Cardinal ....

Fixed ....

Mutable ....

Mutual Reception:

Unaspected:

Retrograde:

Other chart points:

Sign emphasis:

House emphasis:

Singletons/Duets:

Equal Houses

Placidus Houses

ASPECTS & CONFIGURATIONS

THEMES & OTHER OBSERVATIONS

Born 20 May 1946, 07:25 PST (+8)
El Centro, California, USA (32n48, 115w34)

Source: Birth certificate quoted in 'Contemporary American
Horoscopes'. (Salvatore Phillip 'Sonny' Bono was born 16
February 1935, 21:21 EST (+5), Detroit, Michigan (42n20,
83w03). Same source.)
RR: AA
(Cheryl LaPiere)
Data Collector: Janice Mackay-Saunders

Notes:

DEEPAK CHOPRA

Doctor; writer on spirituality, mind-body medicine, God
and the afterlife; author of *The Seven Spiritual Laws of Success*

Sun ....

Moon ....

Ascendant ....

     Chart Ruler ....

Fire ....

Earth ....

Air ....

Water ....

Cardinal ....

Fixed ....

Mutable ....

Mutual Reception: Sign emphasis:

Unaspected: House emphasis:

Retrograde: Singletons/Duets:

Other chart points:

Equal Houses

Placidus Houses

ASPECTS & CONFIGURATIONS

THEMES & OTHER OBSERVATIONS

Born 22 October 1946, 15:45 IST (-5.5)
New Delhi, India (28n36, 77e12)

Source: From him to Linda Clark. The Chopra Centre sent a
Vedic chart to subscribers with a time of 15:51.

RR: A
                      (Deepak Chopra)
                      Data Collector: Linda Clark

Notes:

WINSTON CHURCHILL

Statesman, historian and inspired orator; UK's Prime
Minister from 10/5/1940 to 27/7/1945; 26/10/1951 to 7/4/1955

Sun ....

Moon ....

Ascendant ....

    Chart Ruler ....

Fire ....

Earth ....

Air ....

Water ....

Cardinal ....

Fixed ....

Mutable ....

Mutual Reception: Sign emphasis:

Unaspected: House emphasis:

Retrograde: Singletons/Duets:

Other chart points:

Equal Houses

Placidus Houses

ASPECTS & CONFIGURATIONS

THEMES & OTHER OBSERVATIONS

Born 30 November 1874, 01:30 GMT (+0)
Blenheim Palace, Woodstock, England (51n50, 1w22)

Source: Father's letter (on the day of Winston's birth)
quoted by son Randolph in a biography on his father, 'Youth
1874-1900'.

RR: A   (Winston Leonard Spencer Churchill)
                        Data Collector: Arthur Blackwell

Notes:

BILL CLINTON

Governor of Arkansas (9/1/1979 to 19/1/1981; 11/1/1983 to
12/12/1992); US President (20/1/1993 to 20/1/2001)

Sun ....

Moon ....

Ascendant ....

    Chart Ruler ....

Fire ....

Earth ....

Air ....

Water ....

Cardinal ....

Fixed ....

Mutable ....

Mutual Reception: Sign emphasis:

Unaspected: House emphasis:

Retrograde: Singletons/Duets:

Other chart points:

Equal Houses

Placidus Houses

ASPECTS & CONFIGURATIONS

THEMES & OTHER OBSERVATIONS

Born 19 August 1946, 08:51 CST (+6)
Hope, Arkansas, USA (33n40, 93w35)

Source: Note from Clinton's mother to Shelley Ackerman, copy
on file.

RR: A

(William Jefferson Blythe IV)
Data Collector: Shelley Ackerman

Notes:

KURT COBAIN

Lead singer-guitarist for grunge band Nirvana; mainstream
success from 9/1991; met Courtney Love on 12/1/1990

Sun ....

Moon ....

Ascendant ....

      Chart Ruler ....

Fire ....

Earth ....

Air ....

Water ....

Cardinal ....

Fixed ....

Mutable ....

Mutual Reception: Sign emphasis:

Unaspected: House emphasis:

Retrograde: Singletons/Duets:

Other chart points:

Equal Houses

Placidus Houses

ASPECTS & CONFIGURATIONS

THEMES & OTHER OBSERVATIONS

Born 20 February 1967, 19:20 PST (+8)
Aberdeen, Washington, USA (46n59, 123w49)

Source: Cobain's mother to Muriel Foltz. (Wife Courtney Love
was born Courtney Michelle Harrison on 9 July 1964, 14:08
PDT (+7), San Francisco, California, USA (37n47, 122w25).
Birth certificate from her astrologer Nancy Hastings.)
RR: A   (Kurt Donald Cobain)
Data Collector: Muriel Foltz

Notes:

SALVADOR DALÍ

Eccentric Surrealist painter, sculptor, writer and self-
publicist; noted for his flamboyant, iconic moustache

Sun ....

Moon ....

Ascendant ....

     Chart Ruler ....

Fire ....

Earth ....

Air ....

Water ....

Cardinal ....

Fixed ....

Mutable ....

Mutual Reception: Sign emphasis:

Unaspected: House emphasis:

Retrograde: Singletons/Duets:

Other chart points:

Equal Houses

Placidus Houses

ASPECTS & CONFIGURATIONS

THEMES & OTHER OBSERVATIONS

Born 11 May 1904, 08:45 GMT (+0)
Figueras, Spain (42n16, 2e58)

Source: Note from birth registry, copy on file; same on birth
certificate.

RR: AA   (Salvador Felipe Jacinto Dalí i Domenech)
     Data Collector: Juan Trigo

Notes:

JOHN DELOREAN

Automobile industry executive; founded the DeLorean
Motor Company on 24/10/1975 (in receivership by 2/1982)

Sun ....

Moon ....

Ascendant ....

     Chart Ruler ....

Fire ....

Earth ....

Air ....

Water ....

Cardinal ....

Fixed ....

Mutable ....

Mutual Reception: Sign emphasis:

Unaspected: House emphasis:

Retrograde: Singletons/Duets:

Other chart points:

Equal Houses

Placidus Houses

ASPECTS & CONFIGURATIONS

THEMES & OTHER OBSERVATIONS

Born 6 January 1925, 12:00 EST (+5)
Detroit, Michigan, USA (42n20, 83w03)

Source: Birth certificate.

RR: AA

(John Zachary DeLorean)
Data Collectors: M. and F. Gauquelin

Notes:

JOHNNY DEPP

Actor known for playing offbeat, eccentric characters on
film; sex symbol since TV's *21 Jump Street* (prem. 12/4/1987)

Sun ....

Moon ....

Ascendant ....

      Chart Ruler ....

Fire ....

Earth ....

Air ....

Water ....

Cardinal ....

Fixed ....

Mutable ....

Mutual Reception: Sign emphasis:

Unaspected: House emphasis:

Retrograde: Singletons/Duets:

Other chart points:

Equal Houses

Placidus Houses

ASPECTS & CONFIGURATIONS

THEMES & OTHER OBSERVATIONS

Born 9 June 1963, 08:44 CST (+6)
Owensboro, Kentucky, USA (37n46, 87w07)

Source: Hospital birth certificate, copy on file.

RR: AA

(John Christopher Depp II)
Data Collector: Edwin Steinbrecher

Notes:

PRINCESS DIANA

Princess of Wales; officially engaged to Charles on 24/2/1981,
married 29/7/1981, separated 9/12/1992; died 31/8/1997

Sun ....

Moon ....

Ascendant ....

     Chart Ruler ....

Fire ....

Earth ....

Air ....

Water ....

Cardinal ....

Fixed ....

Mutable ....

Mutual Reception: Sign emphasis:

Unaspected: House emphasis:

Retrograde: Singletons/Duets:

Other chart points:

Equal Houses

Placidus Houses

ASPECTS & CONFIGURATIONS

THEMES & OTHER OBSERVATIONS

Born 1 July 1961, 19:45 GDT (-1)
Sandringham, England (52n50, 0e30)

Source: Her mother; same from Diana to her astrologer-friend
Debbie Frank. Although Buckingham Palace originally released
a time of '2pm', birth times and anecdotes given later by
Diana appear to have been 'red herrings'.
RR: A
     (Diana Frances Spencer)
Data Collectors: Charles Harvey; Debbie Frank

Notes:

LEONARDO DiCAPRIO

Actor who achieved international stardom ('Leo-mania') in
the blockbuster film *Titanic* (US prem. 19/12/1997)

Sun ....

Moon ....

Ascendant ....

      Chart Ruler ....

Fire ....

Earth ....

Air ....

Water ....

Cardinal ....

Fixed ....

Mutable ....

Mutual Reception: Sign emphasis:

Unaspected: House emphasis:

Retrograde: Singletons/Duets:

Other chart points:

Equal Houses

Placidus Houses

ASPECTS & CONFIGURATIONS

THEMES & OTHER OBSERVATIONS

Born 11 November 1974, 02:47 PST (+8)
Los Angeles, California, USA (34n03, 118w15)

Source: Birth certificate, copy on file.

RR: AA

(Leonardo Wilhelm DiCaprio)
Data Collector: Frank Clifford

Notes:

MARLENE DIETRICH

Sensual, androgynous actress and cabaret artist; famous
upon the release of *The Blue Angel* (German prem. 1/4/1930)

Sun ....

Moon ....

Ascendant ....

    Chart Ruler ....

Fire ....

Earth ....

Air ....

Water ....

Cardinal ....

Fixed ....

Mutable ....

Mutual Reception: Sign emphasis:

Unaspected: House emphasis:

Retrograde: Singletons/Duets:

Other chart points:

Equal Houses

Placidus Houses

ASPECTS & CONFIGURATIONS

THEMES & OTHER OBSERVATIONS

Born 27 December 1901, 21:15 MET (-1)
Berlin-Schöneberg, Germany (52n28, 13e22)

Source: Note from birth registry, copy on file.

RR: AA

(Marie Magdalene Dietrich)
Data Collector: Luc DeMarre

Notes:

WALT DISNEY

Innovative, pioneering animator; film producer, director, screenwriter; visionary entrepreneur of Disneyland (opened 17/7/1955)

Sun ....

Moon ....

Ascendant ....

    Chart Ruler ....

Fire ....

Earth ....

Air ....

Water ....

Cardinal ....

Fixed ....

Mutable ....

Mutual Reception:

Unaspected:

Retrograde:

Other chart points:

Sign emphasis:

House emphasis:

Singletons/Duets:

Equal Houses

Placidus Houses

ASPECTS & CONFIGURATIONS

THEMES & OTHER OBSERVATIONS

Born 5 December 1901, 00:35 CST (+6)
Chicago, Illinois, USA (41n51 87w39)

Source: Disney Studio office to Marion March.

RR: A

(Walter Elias Disney)
Data Collector: Marion March

Notes:

ARTHUR CONAN DOYLE

Writer of science fiction and historical novels; creator of the
detective Sherlock Holmes (pub. from 12/1887); spiritualist

Sun ....

Moon ....

Ascendant ....

      Chart Ruler ....

Fire ....

Earth ....

Air ....

Water ....

Cardinal ....

Fixed ....

Mutable ....

Mutual Reception: Sign emphasis:

Unaspected: House emphasis:

Retrograde: Singletons/Duets:

Other chart points:

Equal Houses

Placidus Houses

ASPECTS & CONFIGURATIONS

THEMES & OTHER OBSERVATIONS

Notes:

Born 22 May 1859, 04:55 GMT (+0)
Edinburgh, Scotland (55n57, 3w13)

Source: Birth certificate, copy on file.

RR: AA

(Arthur Conan Doyle)
Data Collector: Paul Wright

BOB DYLAN

Highly influential singer-songwriter; fused poetry with
anthemic music; chronicled the social unrest of his generation

Sun ....

Moon ....

Ascendant ....

      Chart Ruler ....

Fire ....

Earth ....

Air ....

Water ....

Cardinal ....

Fixed ....

Mutable ....

Mutual Reception: Sign emphasis:

Unaspected: House emphasis:

Retrograde: Singletons/Duets:

Other chart points:

Equal Houses

Placidus Houses

ASPECTS & CONFIGURATIONS

THEMES & OTHER OBSERVATIONS

Born 24 May 1941, 21:05 CST (+6)
Duluth, Minnesota, USA (46n47, 92w06)

Source: Birth certificate, copy on file.

RR: AA   (Robert Allen Zimmerman)
                        Data Collector: Bob Garner

Notes:

AMELIA EARHART

Aviation pioneer; the first woman to fly solo across the
Atlantic (20/5/1932); mysterious disappearance on 2/7/1937

Sun ....

Moon ....

Ascendant ....

      Chart Ruler ....

Fire ....

Earth ....

Air ....

Water ....

Cardinal ....

Fixed ....

Mutable ....

Mutual Reception: Sign emphasis:

Unaspected: House emphasis:

Retrograde: Singletons/Duets:

Other chart points:

Equal Houses

Placidus Houses

ASPECTS & CONFIGURATIONS

THEMES & OTHER OBSERVATIONS

Born 24 July 1897, 23:30 CST (+6)
Atchison, Kansas, USA (39n34, 95w07)

Source: From her to Mrs Yerington, when Earhart was a guest
lecturer at the National Women's Party.

RR: A

(Amelia Mary Earhart)
Data Collector: Gene Lockhart

Notes:

ALBERT EINSTEIN

Physicist, known for his theories of relativity and mass-
energy equivalence theory (E=MC²); Nobel Prize (9/11/1922)

Sun ....

Moon ....

Ascendant ....

      Chart Ruler ....

Fire ....

Earth ....

Air ....

Water ....

Cardinal ....

Fixed ....

Mutable ....

Mutual Reception: Sign emphasis:

Unaspected: House emphasis:

Retrograde: Singletons/Duets:

Other chart points:

Equal Houses

Placidus Houses

ASPECTS & CONFIGURATIONS

THEMES & OTHER OBSERVATIONS

Born 14 March 1879, 11:30 LMT (-0:40:00)
Ulm, Germany (48n24, 10e00)

Source: Birth record, copy on file.

RR: AA   (Albert Einstein)
Data Collector: Reinhold Ebertin

Notes:

GEORGE ELIOT

Victorian author who used a male pen name; scandal from
living with her male lover; *Middlemarch* (first part pub. 12/1871)

Sun ....

Moon ....

Ascendant ....

    Chart Ruler ....

Fire ....

Earth ....

Air ....

Water ....

Cardinal ....

Fixed ....

Mutable ....

Mutual Reception: Sign emphasis:

Unaspected: House emphasis:

Retrograde: Singletons/Duets:

Other chart points:

Equal Houses

Placidus Houses

ASPECTS & CONFIGURATIONS

THEMES & OTHER OBSERVATIONS

Born 22 November 1819, 05:00 LMT (+0:05:52)
Chilvers Coton, Nuneaton, England (52n31, 1w28)

Source: Father's diary quoted in 'The Complete Works of
George Eliot — Life and Letters'. (Her baptismal certificate
confirms her birth name.)

RR: AA

(Mary Anne Evans)
Data Collector: Gene Lockhart

Notes:

QUEEN ELIZABETH I

'Virgin Queen' from 17/11/1558 to 24/3/1603 OS, an era of seafaring
prowess and theatre; ruled with caution, cunning, political savvy

Sun ....

Moon ....

Ascendant ....

      Chart Ruler ....

Fire ....

Earth ....

Air ....

Water ....

Cardinal ....

Fixed ....

Mutable ....

Mutual Reception: Sign emphasis:

Unaspected: House emphasis:

Retrograde: Singletons/Duets:

Other chart points:

Equal Houses

Placidus Houses

ASPECTS & CONFIGURATIONS

THEMES & OTHER OBSERVATIONS

Born 17 September 1533, 15:00 LAT (-0:05:41)
Greenwich, England (51n29, 0w00)

Source: Latin records quoted in 'Nativitas I' by Martin
Harvey. (7 September Old Style calendar.)

RR: AA   (Elizabeth Tudor)
                           Data Collector: Martin Harvey

Notes:

QUEEN ELIZABETH II

Heiress presumptive from 11/12/1936; became Queen 6/2/1952;
coronation 2/6/1953; strong sense of civic and religious duty

Sun ....

Moon ....

Ascendant ....

    Chart Ruler ....

Fire ....

Earth ....

Air ....

Water ....

Cardinal ....

Fixed ....

Mutable ....

Mutual Reception: Sign emphasis:

Unaspected: House emphasis:

Retrograde: Singletons/Duets:

Other chart points:

ASPECTS & CONFIGURATIONS

THEMES & OTHER OBSERVATIONS

Equal Houses

Placidus Houses

Born 21 April 1926, 02:40 GDT (-1)
Mayfair, London, England (51n31, 0w09)

Source: Official announcement from the Home Office. (Her
consort Prince Philip was born 10 June 1921, 21:46 EET (-2),
Corfu, Greece (39n40, 19e42). Official bulletin.)

RR: A   (Elizabeth Alexandra Mary Windsor)
                          Data Collectors: Cyril Fagan; R.C. Firebrace

Notes:

FARRAH FAWCETT

Actress, model, sex symbol; swimsuit poster and role in TV's
Charlie's Angels (both 9/1976) influenced 70s hair and fashion

Sun ....

Moon ....

Ascendant ....

     Chart Ruler ....

Fire ....

Earth ....

Air ....

Water ....

Cardinal ....

Fixed ....

Mutable ....

Mutual Reception: Sign emphasis:

Unaspected: House emphasis:

Retrograde: Singletons/Duets:

Other chart points:

Equal Houses

Placidus Houses

ASPECTS & CONFIGURATIONS

THEMES & OTHER OBSERVATIONS

Born 2 February 1947, 15:10 CST (+6)
Corpus Christi, Texas, USA (27n48, 97w24)

Source: Birth certificate printed in 'Farrah' by Patricia
Burstein.

RR: AA

(Ferrah Leni Fawcett)
Data Collector: Lois Rodden

Notes:

ROGER FEDERER

Tennis singles champion; joined ATP Tour in 7/1998;
record-setting World #1 (2/2/2004 to 17/8/2008)

Sun ....

Moon ....

Ascendant ....

      Chart Ruler ....

Fire ....

Earth ....

Air ....

Water ....

Cardinal ....

Fixed ....

Mutable ....

Mutual Reception:

Unaspected:

Retrograde:

Other chart points:

Sign emphasis:

House emphasis:

Singletons/Duets:

Equal Houses

Placidus Houses

ASPECTS & CONFIGURATIONS

THEMES & OTHER OBSERVATIONS

Born 8 August 1981, 08:40 MEDT (-2)
Basel, Switzerland (47n33, 7e35)

Source: Federer's official website.

RR: B

(Roger Federer)
Data Collector: David Hamblin

Notes:

F. SCOTT FITZGERALD

Novelist, short story writer; works epitomized the hedonistic
Jazz Age and disillusioned 'Lost Generation'; alcoholic

Sun ....

Moon ....

Ascendant ....

     Chart Ruler ....

Fire ....

Earth ....

Air ....

Water ....

Cardinal ....

Fixed ....

Mutable ....

Mutual Reception: Sign emphasis:

Unaspected: House emphasis:

Retrograde: Singletons/Duets:

Other chart points:

Equal Houses

Placidus Houses

ASPECTS & CONFIGURATIONS

THEMES & OTHER OBSERVATIONS

Born 24 September 1896, 15:30 LMT (+6:12:24)
St Paul, Minnesota, USA (44n57, 93w06)

Source: Biographies 'Exiles from Paradise' by Sara Mayfield
(1971) and 'F. Scott Fitzgerald' by A. Turnbull (1962).

RR: B   (Francis Scott Key Fitzgerald)
    Data Collectors: Ruth Hale Oliver; Arthur Blackwell

Notes:

HEIDI FLEISS

'Hollywood Madame' to the powerful and famous; arrested
6/1993; trials 12/1994 and 5/1995; prison 9/1996 to 11/1998

Sun ....

Moon ....

Ascendant ....

      Chart Ruler ....

Fire ....

Earth ....

Air ....

Water ....

Cardinal ....

Fixed ....

Mutable ....

Mutual Reception: Sign emphasis:

Unaspected: House emphasis:

Retrograde: Singletons/Duets:

Other chart points:

Equal Houses

Placidus Houses

ASPECTS & CONFIGURATIONS

THEMES & OTHER OBSERVATIONS

Born 30 December 1965, 09:05 PST (+8)
Los Angeles, California, USA (34n03, 118w15)

Source: Birth certificate, copy on file.

RR: AA   (Heidi Lynne Fleiss)
Data Collector: Frank Clifford

Notes:

JANE FONDA

Actress, exercise guru and entrepreneur; controversial
political activist ('Hanoi Jane' after a visit there in July 1972)

Sun ....

Moon ....

Ascendant ....

    Chart Ruler ....

Fire ....

Earth ....

Air ....

Water ....

Cardinal ....

Fixed ....

Mutable ....

Mutual Reception: Sign emphasis:

Unaspected: House emphasis:

Retrograde: Singletons/Duets:

Other chart points:

Equal Houses

Placidus Houses

ASPECTS & CONFIGURATIONS

THEMES & OTHER OBSERVATIONS

Born 21 December 1937, 09:14 EST (+5)
Manhattan, New York, USA (40n46, 73w59)

Source: Birth certificate, copy on file.

RR: AA

(Jayne Seymour Fonda)
Data Collector: Lois Rodden

Notes:

HARRISON FORD

Actor best known for *Star Wars* trilogy (from 25/5/1977),
Indiana Jones film series (from 12/6/1981) and *Blade Runner*

Sun ....

Moon ....

Ascendant ....

     Chart Ruler ....

Fire ....

Earth ....

Air ....

Water ....

Cardinal ....

Fixed ....

Mutable ....

Mutual Reception: Sign emphasis:

Unaspected: House emphasis:

Retrograde: Singletons/Duets:

Other chart points:

Equal Houses

Placidus Houses

ASPECTS & CONFIGURATIONS

THEMES & OTHER OBSERVATIONS

Born 13 July 1942, 11:41 CWT (+5)
Chicago, Illinois, USA (41n51, 87w39)

Source: Birth certificate, copy on file.

RR: AA

(Harrison Ford)
Data Collector: Barbara Frigillana

Notes:

JODIE FOSTER

Award-winning actress, director, producer; former child star
(*Taxi Driver*, 8/2/1976); discreet private life, intense, bossy

Sun ....

Moon ....

Ascendant ....

       Chart Ruler ....

Fire ....

Earth ....

Air ....

Water ....

Cardinal ....

Fixed ....

Mutable ....

Mutual Reception: Sign emphasis:

Unaspected: House emphasis:

Retrograde: Singletons/Duets:

Other chart points:

Equal Houses

Placidus Houses

ASPECTS & CONFIGURATIONS

THEMES & OTHER OBSERVATIONS

Born 19 November 1962, 08:14 PST (+8)
Los Angeles, California, USA (34n03, 118w15)

Source: Birth certificate, copy on file.

RR: AA   (Alicia Christina Foster)
Data Collectors: Tom and Thelma Wilson

Notes:

ANNE FRANK

Diarist (12/6/1942 to 1/8/1944); pub. posthumously by her
father on 25/6/1947; a singular voice of courage during WWII

Sun ....

Moon ....

Ascendant ....

    Chart Ruler ....

Fire ....

Earth ....

Air ....

Water ....

Cardinal ....

Fixed ....

Mutable ....

Mutual Reception: Sign emphasis:

Unaspected: House emphasis:

Retrograde: Singletons/Duets:

Other chart points:

Equal Houses

Placidus Houses

ASPECTS & CONFIGURATIONS

THEMES & OTHER OBSERVATIONS

Born 12 June 1929, 07:30 MET (-1)
Frankfurt am Main, Germany (50n07, 8e40)

Source: Baby book from the Anne Frank Museum and Archives in
Amsterdam.

RR: AA

(Annelies Marie Frank)
Data Collector: Becky Altschuler

Notes:

ARETHA FRANKLIN

'Queen of Soul'; powerful gospel-soul-pop singer; signed a
record deal in 8/1960; commercial recognition from 3/1967

Sun ....

Moon ....

Ascendant ....

     Chart Ruler ....

Fire ....

Earth ....

Air ....

Water ....

Cardinal ....

Fixed ....

Mutable ....

Mutual Reception: Sign emphasis:

Unaspected: House emphasis:

Retrograde: Singletons/Duets:

Other chart points:

Equal Houses

Placidus Houses

ASPECTS & CONFIGURATIONS

THEMES & OTHER OBSERVATIONS

Born 25 March 1942, 22:30 CWT (+5)
Memphis, Tennessee, USA (35n09, 90w03)

Source: Birth certificate, copy on file.

RR: AA   (Aretha Louise Franklin)
Data Collector: Edwin Steinbrecher

Notes:

SIGMUND FREUD

Father of modern psychoanalysis; influential theories on the
unconscious mind, repression, transference, 'Oedipus Complex'

Sun ....

Moon ....

Ascendant ....

      Chart Ruler ....

Fire ....

Earth ....

Air ....

Water ....

Cardinal ....

Fixed ....

Mutable ....

Mutual Reception:

Unaspected:

Retrograde:

Other chart points:

Sign emphasis:

House emphasis:

Singletons/Duets:

Equal Houses

Placidus Houses

ASPECTS & CONFIGURATIONS

THEMES & OTHER OBSERVATIONS

Born 6 May 1856, 18:30 LMT (Prague Time -0:57:44)
Freiberg, Moravia (now Príbor, Czech Republic)
(49n38, 18e09)

Source: Father's diary (written in Hebrew and German).

RR: AA

(Sigismund Freud)
Data Collector: Philip Lucas

Notes:

GEORGE GALLOWAY

Confrontational socialist politician; expelled from Labour
Party 10/2003; MP for RESPECT 5/5/2005 (co-founder 1/2004)

Sun ....

Moon ....

Ascendant ....

      Chart Ruler ....

Fire ....

Earth ....

Air ....

Water ....

Cardinal ....

Fixed ....

Mutable ....

Mutual Reception: Sign emphasis:

Unaspected: House emphasis:

Retrograde: Singletons/Duets:

Other chart points:

Equal Houses

Placidus Houses

ASPECTS & CONFIGURATIONS

THEMES & OTHER OBSERVATIONS

Born 16 August 1954, 06:00 GDT (-1)
Dundee, Scotland (56n28, 3w00)

Source: Birth certificate.

RR: AA

(George Galloway)
Data Collector: Caroline Gerard

Notes:

GRETA GARBO

Enigmatic, reclusive star of the silent film era; career from 7/1922;
Hollywood career from 10/9/1925; gradual retirement from 1942

Sun ....

Moon ....

Ascendant ....

      Chart Ruler ....

Fire ....

Earth ....

Air ....

Water ....

Cardinal ....

Fixed ....

Mutable ....

Mutual Reception: Sign emphasis:

Unaspected: House emphasis:

Retrograde: Singletons/Duets:

Other chart points:

Equal Houses

Placidus Houses

ASPECTS & CONFIGURATIONS

THEMES & OTHER OBSERVATIONS

Born 18 September 1905, 19:30 MET (-1)
Stockholm, Sweden (59n20, 18e03)

Source: Two notes from birth registry, both copies on file.
(One typed note states 'Lovisa' — the acknowledged spelling,
the other 'Louisa'.)

RR: AA

(Greta Lovisa Gustafsson)
Data Collector: Ivan Wilhelm

Notes:

JUDY GARLAND

Iconic singer-actress; plagued by addiction and financial
crises; won role in *The Wizard of Oz* 2/1938, prem. 15/8/1939

Sun ....

Moon ....

Ascendant ....

      Chart Ruler ....

Fire ....

Earth ....

Air ....

Water ....

Cardinal ....

Fixed ....

Mutable ....

Mutual Reception: Sign emphasis:

Unaspected: House emphasis:

Retrograde: Singletons/Duets:

Other chart points:

Equal Houses

Placidus Houses

ASPECTS & CONFIGURATIONS

THEMES & OTHER OBSERVATIONS

Notes:

Born 10 June 1922, 06:00 CST (+6)
Grand Rapids, Minnesota, USA (47n14, 93w32)

Source: Note from birth registry, copy on file; birth
certificate quoted in 'Contemporary American Horoscopes'.
Scott Schechter's thorough biography 'Judy Garland' (Cooper
Square Press, 2002) gives 05:30.
RR: AA   (Frances Ethel Gumm)
  Data Collectors: Edwin Steinbrecher; Janice Mackay-Saunders

LINDA GOODMAN

Top-selling astrology author of all time; *Sun Signs* pub.
6/1968; also wrote on numerology, lexigrams and immortality

Sun ....

Moon ....

Ascendant ....

      Chart Ruler ....

Fire ....

Earth ....

Air ....

Water ....

Cardinal ....

Fixed ....

Mutable ....

Mutual Reception: Sign emphasis:

Unaspected: House emphasis:

Retrograde: Singletons/Duets:

Other chart points:

Equal Houses

Placidus Houses

ASPECTS & CONFIGURATIONS

THEMES & OTHER OBSERVATIONS

Born 9 April 1925, 06:05 EST (+5)
Morgantown, West Virginia, USA (39n38, 79w57)

Source: Birth certificate, copy on file. Same data and
Ascendant degree given online by Goodman's confidante BiBi
DeAngelo, except with a time of 06:15 in error.

RR: AA

(Mary Alice Kemery)
Data Collector: Frank Clifford

Notes:

PRINCESS GRACE OF MONACO

Glamorous, elegant Hollywood actress; fairytale princess;
met Prince Rainier of Monaco 6/5/1955, married 19/4/1956

Sun ....

Moon ....

Ascendant ....

      Chart Ruler ....

Fire ....

Earth ....

Air ....

Water ....

Cardinal ....

Fixed ....

Mutable ....

Mutual Reception: Sign emphasis:

Unaspected: House emphasis:

Retrograde: Singletons/Duets:

Other chart points:

Equal Houses

Placidus Houses

ASPECTS & CONFIGURATIONS

THEMES & OTHER OBSERVATIONS

Born 12 November 1929, 05:31 EST (+5)
Philadelphia, Pennsylvania, USA (39n57, 75w10)

Source: Birth certificate, copy on file. (Husband Prince
Rainier III of Monaco was born 31 May 1923, 06:00 GDT (-1),
Monte Carlo, Monaco (43n45, 7e25). Official announcement.)

RR: AA

                            (Grace Patricia Kelly)
                            Data Collector: Bob Garner

Notes:

STEFFI GRAF

Tennis champion, supreme on all surfaces; World #1 from
17/8/1987; 'Golden' Slam 1988; married Andre Agassi 22/10/2001

Sun ....

Moon ....

Ascendant ....

     Chart Ruler ....

Fire ....

Earth ....

Air ....

Water ....

Cardinal ....

Fixed ....

Mutable ....

Mutual Reception: Sign emphasis:

Unaspected: House emphasis:

Retrograde: Singletons/Duets:

Other chart points:

Equal Houses

Placidus Houses

ASPECTS & CONFIGURATIONS

THEMES & OTHER OBSERVATIONS

Born 14 June 1969, 04:40 MET (-1)
Mannheim, Germany (49n29, 8e29)

Source: Birth record.

RR: AA

(Stefanie Maria Graf)
Data Collector: Hans Hinrich Taeger

Notes:

GERMAINE GREER

Writer, journalist, academic; highly influential feminist
spokeswoman upon the release of *The Female Eunuch* 10/1970

Sun ....

Moon ....

Ascendant ....

      Chart Ruler ....

Fire ....

Earth ....

Air ....

Water ....

Cardinal ....

Fixed ....

Mutable ....

Mutual Reception: Sign emphasis:

Unaspected: House emphasis:

Retrograde: Singletons/Duets:

Other chart points:

Equal Houses

Placidus Houses

ASPECTS & CONFIGURATIONS

THEMES & OTHER OBSERVATIONS

Born 29 January 1939, 06:00 AEST (-10)
Melbourne, Australia (37s49, 144e58)

Source: From her to Tiffany Holmes.

RR: A   (Germaine Greer)
        Data Collector: Tiffany Holmes

Notes:

FLORENCE GRIFFITH-JOYNER

'Flo-Jo'; controversial, flamboyant, record-shattering
sprinter; three Olympic gold medals in Seoul (9/1988)

Sun ....

Moon ....

Ascendant ....

      Chart Ruler ....

Fire ....

Earth ....

Air ....

Water ....

Cardinal ....

Fixed ....

Mutable ....

Mutual Reception: Sign emphasis:

Unaspected: House emphasis:

Retrograde: Singletons/Duets:

Other chart points:

Equal Houses

Placidus Houses

ASPECTS & CONFIGURATIONS

THEMES & OTHER OBSERVATIONS

Born 21 December 1959, 00:11 PST (+8)
Los Angeles, California, USA (34n03, 118w15)

Source: Birth certificate, copy on file.

RR: AA

(Florence Delorez Griffith)
Data Collector: Frank Clifford

Notes:

ALEX HALEY

Bestselling author of *Roots* (17/8/1976) and *The Autobiography of Malcolm X* (29/10/1965); *Roots* TV mini-series telecast 1/1977

Sun ....

Moon ....

Ascendant ....

     Chart Ruler ....

Fire ....

Earth ....

Air ....

Water ....

Cardinal ....

Fixed ....

Mutable ....

Mutual Reception: Sign emphasis:

Unaspected: House emphasis:

Retrograde: Singletons/Duets:

Other chart points:

Equal Houses

Placidus Houses

ASPECTS & CONFIGURATIONS

THEMES & OTHER OBSERVATIONS

Born 11 August 1921, 04:55 EDT (+4)
Ithaca, New York, USA (42n26, 76w30)

Source: Birth certificate quoted in 'Contemporary American Horoscopes'.

RR: AA

(Alexander Murray Palmer Haley)
Data Collector: Janice Mackay-Saunders

Notes:

THOMAS HARDY

Novelist with an eye for poignant detail; attacked for atheism,
immorality; his rural characters struggled against their passions

Sun ....

Moon ....

Ascendant ....

      Chart Ruler ....

Fire ....

Earth ....

Air ....

Water ....

Cardinal ....

Fixed ....

Mutable ....

Mutual Reception: Sign emphasis:

Unaspected: House emphasis:

Retrograde: Singletons/Duets:

Other chart points:

Equal Houses

Placidus Houses

ASPECTS & CONFIGURATIONS

THEMES & OTHER OBSERVATIONS

Born 2 June 1840, 08:00 LMT (+0:09:32)
Higher Bockhampton, England (50n44, 2w23)

Source: Biography (largely co-written with Hardy) by his
wife Florence Emily Hardy, 'The Early Life of Thomas Hardy'
(Macmillan, 1928), 'about 8 am'.

RR: B   (Thomas Hardy)
Data Collector: Paul Wright

Notes:

LEONA HELMSLEY

'Queen of Mean'; billionaire hotelier/realtor upon marriage
on 8/4/1972; tax evasion scandal 3/12/1986; convicted 8/1989

Sun ....

Moon ....

Ascendant ....

      Chart Ruler ....

Fire ....

Earth ....

Air ....

Water ....

Cardinal ....

Fixed ....

Mutable ....

Mutual Reception: Sign emphasis:

Unaspected: House emphasis:

Retrograde: Singletons/Duets:

Other chart points:

Equal Houses

Placidus Houses

ASPECTS & CONFIGURATIONS

THEMES & OTHER OBSERVATIONS

Born 4 July 1920, 06:00 EDT (+4)
High Falls, Marbletown, New York, USA (41n50, 74w08)

Source: Birth certificate quoted in 'Palace Coup' by Michael
Moss (Doubleday, 1989), p.33, copy on file. (Known as Leona
Mindy Rosenthal.) (Husband Harry Helmsley was born 4 March
1909, New York. Birth certificate, copy on file. No time.)
RR: AA   (Lena Rosenthol)
Data Collector: Frank Clifford

Notes:

JIMI HENDRIX

Legendary, pioneering, creative guitarist; synthesized styles
to create a unique musical form; US fame from 18/6/1967

Sun ....

Moon ....

Ascendant ....

      Chart Ruler ....

Fire ....

Earth ....

Air ....

Water ....

Cardinal ....

Fixed ....

Mutable ....

Mutual Reception: Sign emphasis:

Unaspected: House emphasis:

Retrograde: Singletons/Duets:

Other chart points:

Equal Houses

Placidus Houses

ASPECTS & CONFIGURATIONS

THEMES & OTHER OBSERVATIONS

Born 27 November 1942, 10:15 PWT (+7)
Seattle, Washington, USA (47n36, 122w20)

Source: Birth certificate, copy on file.

RR: AA   (Johnny Allen Hendrix, later corrected to
James Marshall Hendrix)
Data Collector: Janice Mackay-Saunders

Notes:

MYRA HINDLEY

'Moors Murderer' (7/1963 to 10/1965) with lover Ian Brady
(qv); House of Lords appeals (12/1997, 11/1998, 3/2000) denied

Sun ....

Moon ....

Ascendant ....

      Chart Ruler ....

Fire ....

Earth ....

Air ....

Water ....

Cardinal ....

Fixed ....

Mutable ....

Mutual Reception: Sign emphasis:

Unaspected: House emphasis:

Retrograde: Singletons/Duets:

Other chart points:

Equal Houses

Placidus Houses

ASPECTS & CONFIGURATIONS

THEMES & OTHER OBSERVATIONS

Born 23 July 1942, 02:45 DGWT (-2)
Crumpsall, Lancashire, England (53N31, 2w15)

Source: Biography 'Inside the Mind of a Murderess' by Jean
Ritchie states 'between 2.30 and 3 am'.

RR: B   (Myra Hindley)
      Data Collector: David Fisher

Notes:

ADOLF HITLER

Nazi Party dictator; German Chancellor from 30/1/1933;
invasion of Poland led to World War II (3/9/1939 to 2/9/1945)

Sun ....

Moon ....

Ascendant ....

     Chart Ruler ....

Fire ....

Earth ....

Air ....

Water ....

Cardinal ....

Fixed ....

Mutable ....

Mutual Reception: Sign emphasis:

Unaspected: House emphasis:

Retrograde: Singletons/Duets:

Other chart points:

Equal Houses

Placidus Houses

ASPECTS & CONFIGURATIONS

THEMES & OTHER OBSERVATIONS

Born 20 April 1889, 18:30 LMT (-0:52:08)
Braunau am Inn, Austria (48n15, 13e02)

Source: Church baptismal record.

RR: AA   (Adolf Hitler)
Data Collector: Heinz Noesselt

Notes:

BILLIE HOLIDAY

'Lady Day'; iconic, emotive, distinctive jazz-blues singer and
tragedienne; career spiralled out of control due to drug abuse

Sun ....

Moon ....

Ascendant ....

      Chart Ruler ....

Fire ....

Earth ....

Air ....

Water ....

Cardinal ....

Fixed ....

Mutable ....

Mutual Reception: Sign emphasis:

Unaspected: House emphasis:

Retrograde: Singletons/Duets:

Other chart points:

Equal Houses

Placidus Houses

ASPECTS & CONFIGURATIONS

THEMES & OTHER OBSERVATIONS

Born 7 April 1915, 02:30 EST (+5)
Philadelphia, Pennsylvania, USA (39n57, 75w10)

Source: Birth certificate quoted in Stuart Nicholson's
biography 'Billie Holiday' (Victor Gollancz, 1995), p.18,
copy on file. Same data in Donald Clarke's biography 'Wishing
on the Moon'.
RR: AA   (Elinore Harris, later written 'Eleanora')
      Data Collectors: David Stenn; Frank Clifford

Notes:

WHITNEY HOUSTON

Glamorous singer; reached commercial stratosphere with
debut album (rel. 14/2/1985) and *The Bodyguard*, 25/11/1992

Sun ....

Moon ....

Ascendant ....

      Chart Ruler ....

Fire ....

Earth ....

Air ....

Water ....

Cardinal ....

Fixed ....

Mutable ....

Mutual Reception:

Unaspected:

Retrograde:

Other chart points:

Sign emphasis:

House emphasis:

Singletons/Duets:

Equal Houses

Placidus Houses

ASPECTS & CONFIGURATIONS

THEMES & OTHER OBSERVATIONS

Born 9 August 1963, 20:55 EDT (+4)
Newark, New Jersey, USA (40n44, 74w10)

Source: Birth certificate, copy on file. (Ex-husband Robert
Baresford Brown was born 5 February 1969, 05:21 EST, Boston,
Massachusetts, USA (42n22, 71w04). Birth certificate, copy on
file.)
RR: AA

(Whitney Elizabeth Houston)
Data Collector: Kathryn Farmer

Notes:

ANGELINA JOLIE

Actress; Goodwill Ambassador; star status following *Tomb Raider* (rel. 15/6/2001); high-profile union with Brad Pitt (qv)

Sun ....

Moon ....

Ascendant ....

      Chart Ruler ....

Fire ....

Earth ....

Air ....

Water ....

Cardinal ....

Fixed ....

Mutable ....

Mutual Reception: Sign emphasis:

Unaspected: House emphasis:

Retrograde: Singletons/Duets:

Other chart points:

Equal Houses

Placidus Houses

ASPECTS & CONFIGURATIONS

THEMES & OTHER OBSERVATIONS

Born 4 June 1975, 09:09 PDT (+7)
Los Angeles, California, USA (34n03, 118w15)

Source: Birth certificate.

RR: AA

(Angelina Jolie Voight)
Data Collector: Marc Penfield

Notes:

JIM JONES

'Father' of the integrationist, socialist People's Temple, later
an agricultural community in Guyana; mass suicide 18/11/1978

Sun ....

Moon ....

Ascendant ....

    Chart Ruler ....

Fire ....

Earth ....

Air ....

Water ....

Cardinal ....

Fixed ....

Mutable ....

Mutual Reception: Sign emphasis:

Unaspected: House emphasis:

Retrograde: Singletons/Duets:

Other chart points:

Equal Houses

Placidus Houses

ASPECTS & CONFIGURATIONS

THEMES & OTHER OBSERVATIONS

Born 13 May 1931, 22:00 CST (+6)
Lynn, Indiana, USA (40n03, 84w56)

Source: Date and time from birth registrar to Frank Clifford
by telephone. (Crete, 40n03, 84w52, has also been given.)

RR: AA   (James Warren Jones)
Data Collector: Frank Clifford

Notes:

MARION JONES

Disgraced athlete; stripped of five Olympic medals (won in
9/2000) on 12/12/2007; prison for perjury 7/3–5/9/2008

Sun ....

Moon ....

Ascendant ....

    Chart Ruler ....

Fire ....

Earth ....

Air ....

Water ....

Cardinal ....

Fixed ....

Mutable ....

Mutual Reception: Sign emphasis:

Unaspected: House emphasis:

Retrograde: Singletons/Duets:

Other chart points:

Equal Houses

Placidus Houses

ASPECTS & CONFIGURATIONS

THEMES & OTHER OBSERVATIONS

Born 12 October 1975, 08:01 PDT (+7)
Los Angeles, California, USA (34n03, 118w15)

Source: Birth certificate.

RR: AA

(Marion Lois Jones)
Data Collector: Pat Taglilatelo

Notes:

ERICA JONG

Feminist author of the landmark *Fear of Flying* (1973), an
erotic, taboo-shattering exploration of female sexual desire

Sun ....

Moon ....

Ascendant ....

      Chart Ruler ....

Fire ....

Earth ....

Air ....

Water ....

Cardinal ....

Fixed ....

Mutable ....

Mutual Reception: Sign emphasis:

Unaspected: House emphasis:

Retrograde: Singletons/Duets:

Other chart points:

Equal Houses

Placidus Houses

ASPECTS & CONFIGURATIONS

THEMES & OTHER OBSERVATIONS

Born 26 March 1942, 10:25 EWT (+4)
Manhattan, New York, USA (40n46, 73w59)

Source: Birth certificate, copy on file.

RR: AA   (Erica Mann)
       Data Collectors: Lois Rodden; Janice Mackay-Saunders

Notes:

JANIS JOPLIN

Raw, intense, bluesy singer; a tumultuous, tortured, short
life ending in an accidental drugs overdose on 4/10/1970

Sun ....

Moon ....

Ascendant ....

      Chart Ruler ....

Fire ....

Earth ....

Air ....

Water ....

Cardinal ....

Fixed ....

Mutable ....

Mutual Reception: Sign emphasis:

Unaspected: House emphasis:

Retrograde: Singletons/Duets:

Other chart points:

Equal Houses

Placidus Houses

ASPECTS & CONFIGURATIONS

THEMES & OTHER OBSERVATIONS

Born 19 January 1943, 09:45 CWT (+5)
Port Arthur, Texas, USA (29n54, 93w56)

Source: Birth certificate, copy on file.

RR: AA   (Janis Lyn Joplin)
Data Collector: Frank Clifford

Notes:

CARL GUSTAV JUNG

Psychologist; explored the psyche through archetypes, dreams,
spirituality, mythology; 'collective unconscious', 'synchronicity'

Sun ....

Moon ....

Ascendant ....

      Chart Ruler ....

Fire ....

Earth ....

Air ....

Water ....

Cardinal ....

Fixed ....

Mutable ....

Mutual Reception: Sign emphasis:

Unaspected: House emphasis:

Retrograde: Singletons/Duets:

Other chart points:

ASPECTS & CONFIGURATIONS

THEMES & OTHER OBSERVATIONS

Equal Houses

Placidus Houses

Born 26 July 1875, 19:32 LMT (Berne Time -0:29:44)
Kesswil, Switzerland (47n36, 9e20)
Source: From his daughter, astrologer Gret Baumann, as
quoted in 'Carl Gustav Jung: Leben, Werk, Wirkung' by
Gerhard Wehr (Kosel-Verlag, 1985); most likely rectified by
her. Various other times around sunset have also been given
by Jung and his daughter.
RR: C
                          (Karle Gustav Jung)
                    Data Collector: Lois Rodden

Notes:

CHRISTINE KEELER

Party girl; affairs with British minister John Profumo and
Russian naval attaché scandalized UK politics in 3–10/1963

Sun ....

Moon ....

Ascendant ....

      Chart Ruler ....

Fire ....

Earth ....

Air ....

Water ....

Cardinal ....

Fixed ....

Mutable ....

Mutual Reception: Sign emphasis:

Unaspected: House emphasis:

Retrograde: Singletons/Duets:

Other chart points:

Equal Houses

Placidus Houses

ASPECTS & CONFIGURATIONS

THEMES & OTHER OBSERVATIONS

Born 22 February 1942, 11:15 GDT (−1)
Uxbridge, London, England (51n33, 0w29)

Source: Cyrus Abayakoon vouches for the accuracy of the
data.

RR: A

(Christine Margaret Keeler)
Data Collector: Cyrus Abayakoon

Notes:

JACQUELINE KENNEDY

Enigmatic, stylish US First Lady (20/1/1961 to 22/11/1963);
married shipping tycoon Aristotle Onassis on 20/10/1968

Sun ....

Moon ....

Ascendant ....

      Chart Ruler ....

Fire ....

Earth ....

Air ....

Water ....

Cardinal ....

Fixed ....

Mutable ....

Mutual Reception: Sign emphasis:

Unaspected: House emphasis:

Retrograde: Singletons/Duets:

Other chart points:

Equal Houses

Placidus Houses

ASPECTS & CONFIGURATIONS

THEMES & OTHER OBSERVATIONS

Born 28 July 1929, 14:30 EDT (+4)
Southampton, New York, USA (40n53, 72w23)

Source: From her to mutual friends of Frances McEvoy.

RR: A

(Jacqueline Lee Bouvier)
Data Collector: Frances McEvoy

Notes:

JOHN FITZGERALD KENNEDY

Charismatic 35th US President (from 20/1/1961); political
dynasty and 'Camelot' legacy; assassinated on 22/11/1963

Sun ....

Moon ....

Ascendant ....

     Chart Ruler ....

Fire ....

Earth ....

Air ....

Water ....

Cardinal ....

Fixed ....

Mutable ....

Mutual Reception: Sign emphasis:

Unaspected: House emphasis:

Retrograde: Singletons/Duets:

Other chart points:

Equal Houses

Placidus Houses

ASPECTS & CONFIGURATIONS

THEMES & OTHER OBSERVATIONS

Born 29 May 1917, 15:00 EST (+5)
Brookline, Massachusetts, USA (42n20, 71w07)

Source: From his mother to Garth Allen.

RR: A   (John Fitzgerald Kennedy)
                       Data Collector: Garth Allen

Notes:

MARTIN LUTHER KING, JR

Baptist minister; civil rights activist through non-violence
and civil disobedience; 'I Have a Dream' speech 28/8/1963

Sun ....

Moon ....

Ascendant ....

    Chart Ruler ....

Fire ....

Earth ....

Air ....

Water ....

Cardinal ....

Fixed ....

Mutable ....

Mutual Reception: Sign emphasis:

Unaspected: House emphasis:

Retrograde: Singletons/Duets:

Other chart points:

Equal Houses

Placidus Houses

ASPECTS & CONFIGURATIONS

THEMES & OTHER OBSERVATIONS

Born 15 January 1929, 12:00 CST (+6)
Atlanta, Georgia, USA (33n45, 84w23)

Source: From his mother, 'high noon'. Sy Scholfield quotes
'The Papers of Martin Luther King, Jr' by Clayborne Carson
(et al) (University of California Press, 2005), p. 1, for
'about noon'.
RR: A   (Michael King, Jr; 1930 Census states 'Martin')
    Data Collectors: Ruth Dewey; Sy Scholfield

Notes:

THE KRAY TWINS

Villainous East End thugs during 1950s–60s; nightclub owners;
celebrity friends; arrested 8/5/1968; life sentences on 5/3/1969

Sun ....

Moon ....

Ascendant ....

     Chart Ruler ....

Fire ....

Earth ....

Air ....

Water ....

Cardinal ....

Fixed ....

Mutable ....

Mutual Reception: Sign emphasis:

Unaspected: House emphasis:

Retrograde: Singletons/Duets:

Other chart points:

Equal Houses

Placidus Houses

ASPECTS & CONFIGURATIONS

THEMES & OTHER OBSERVATIONS

Born 24 October 1933, 20:00 GMT (+0)
Hoxton, London, England (51n32, 0e04)

Source: Birth certificates (Reginald at 20:00, Ronald at 20:10).

RR: AA

(Reginald and Ronald Kray)
Data Collector: Ananda Bagley

Notes:

D.H. LAWRENCE

Prolific, passionate novelist, poet and short story writer;
scandalous works probed deep into the human psyche

Sun ....

Moon ....

Ascendant ....

Chart Ruler ....

Fire ....

Earth ....

Air ....

Water ....

Cardinal ....

Fixed ....

Mutable ....

Mutual Reception:

Unaspected:

Retrograde:

Other chart points:

Sign emphasis:

House emphasis:

Singletons/Duets:

Equal Houses

Placidus Houses

ASPECTS & CONFIGURATIONS

THEMES & OTHER OBSERVATIONS

Born 11 September 1885, 09:45 GMT (+0)
Eastwood, England (53n01, 1w18)

Source: From his mother, as given by Professor Therburn.

RR: A

(David Herbert Richards Lawrence)
Data Collector: David Fisher

Notes:

BRUCE LEE

Influential, iconic martial arts master and popular actor; star
in Asia from 10/1971; mysterious early death on 20/7/1973

Sun ....

Moon ....

Ascendant ....

    Chart Ruler ....

Fire ....

Earth ....

Air ....

Water ....

Cardinal ....

Fixed ....

Mutable ....

Equal Houses

Mutual Reception: Sign emphasis:

Unaspected: House emphasis:

Retrograde: Singletons/Duets:

Other chart points:

Placidus Houses

ASPECTS & CONFIGURATIONS

THEMES & OTHER OBSERVATIONS

Born 27 November 1940, 07:12 PST (+8)
San Francisco, California, USA (37n47, 122w25)

Source: Birth certificate, copy on file. (The certificate lists
both English and Chinese versions of his name; it lists his
name as 'Fon' not 'Fan', as used by biographers.)

RR: AA

(Bruce Lee/Li Jun Fon)
Data Collector: Robert Paige

Notes:

MONICA LEWINSKY

Infamous White House intern; intimacy with President Bill
Clinton (qv) from 11/1995 to 3/1997; scandal/Grand Jury 1–9/1998

Sun ....

Moon ....

Ascendant ....

      Chart Ruler ....

Fire ....

Earth ....

Air ....

Water ....

Cardinal ....

Fixed ....

Mutable ....

Mutual Reception: Sign emphasis:

Unaspected: House emphasis:

Retrograde: Singletons/Duets:

Other chart points:

Equal Houses

Placidus Houses

ASPECTS & CONFIGURATIONS

THEMES & OTHER OBSERVATIONS

Born 23 July 1973, 12:21 PDT (+7)
San Francisco, California, USA (37n47, 122w25)

Source: Birth certificate.

RR: AA

(Monica Samille Lewinsky)
Data Collector: Jack Fertig

Notes:

CARL LEWIS

Record-setting sprinter and long jumper; dominance from
6/1981; nine-time Olympic gold medallist (1984–1996)

Sun ....

Moon ....

Ascendant ....

    Chart Ruler ....

Fire ....

Earth ....

Air ....

Water ....

Cardinal ....

Fixed ....

Mutable ....

Mutual Reception: Sign emphasis:

Unaspected: House emphasis:

Retrograde: Singletons/Duets:

Other chart points:

Equal Houses

Placidus Houses

ASPECTS & CONFIGURATIONS

THEMES & OTHER OBSERVATIONS

Born 1 July 1961, 07:49 CST (+6)
Birmingham, Alabama, USA (33n31, 86w48)

Source: Note from Lewis to Mary Frances Wood, copy on file.

RR: A

(Frederick Carlton Lewis)
Data Collector: Mary Frances Wood

Notes:

LIBERACE

Flamboyant showman, pianist and matinée idol; opulent lifestyle from TV/Vegas shows; libelled 9/1956 (won case 6/1959)

Sun ....

Moon ....

Ascendant ....

      Chart Ruler ....

Fire ....

Earth ....

Air ....

Water ....

Cardinal ....

Fixed ....

Mutable ....

Mutual Reception: Sign emphasis:

Unaspected: House emphasis:

Retrograde: Singletons/Duets:

Other chart points:

Equal Houses

Placidus Houses

ASPECTS & CONFIGURATIONS

THEMES & OTHER OBSERVATIONS

Born 16 May 1919, 23:15 CWT (+5)
West Allis, Wisconsin, USA (43n01, 88w00)

Source: Note from birth registry, copy on file; birth
certificate quoted in 'Contemporary Sidereal Horoscopes'.
(Walter, the anglicized version of Wladziu, is on the birth
certificate.)
RR: AA   (Walter Valentino Liberace)
  Data Collectors: Edwin Steinbrecher; Janice Mackay-Saunders

Notes:

GEORGE LUCAS

Independent producer-director; created *Star Wars* film epics
(prem. 25/5/1977; second set from 19/5/1999) and *Indiana Jones*

Sun ....

Moon ....

Ascendant ....

      Chart Ruler ....

Fire ....

Earth ....

Air ....

Water ....

Cardinal ....

Fixed ....

Mutable ....

Mutual Reception: Sign emphasis:

Unaspected: House emphasis:

Retrograde: Singletons/Duets:

Other chart points:

Equal Houses

Placidus Houses

ASPECTS & CONFIGURATIONS

THEMES & OTHER OBSERVATIONS

Born 14 May 1944, 05:40 PWT (+7)
Modesto, California, USA (37n38, 121w00)

Source: Birth certificate, copy on file.

RR: AA

(George Walton Lucas, Jr)
Data Collectors: Edwin Steinbrecher;
M. and F. Gauquelin; Janice Mackay-Saunders

Notes:

MADONNA

Controversial, media-savvy, iconic singer-dancer-actress;
mistress of reinvention; global commercial success from 11/1984

Sun ....

Moon ....

Ascendant ....

     Chart Ruler ....

Fire ....

Earth ....

Air ....

Water ....

Cardinal ....

Fixed ....

Mutable ....

Mutual Reception: Sign emphasis:

Unaspected: House emphasis:

Retrograde: Singletons/Duets:

Other chart points:

Equal Houses

Placidus Houses

ASPECTS & CONFIGURATIONS

THEMES & OTHER OBSERVATIONS

Born 16 August 1958, 07:05 EST (+5)
Bay City, Michigan, USA (43n36, 83w53)

Source: Hospital record, as quoted by Madonna's father, who
called the hospital. Same data in 'Madonna: A Biography' by
Mary Cross (Greenwood, 2007), p.1.

RR: AA   (Madonna Louise Ciccone)
           Data Collectors: Tashi Grady; Sy Scholfield

Notes:

CHARLES MANSON

Notorious head of the 'Manson Family'; attempted to incite race
war; brutal killings 7–8/1969; trial from 15/6/1970; guilty 25/1/1971

Sun ....

Moon ....

Ascendant ....

      Chart Ruler ....

Fire ....

Earth ....

Air ....

Water ....

Cardinal ....

Fixed ....

Mutable ....

Mutual Reception: Sign emphasis:

Unaspected: House emphasis:

Retrograde: Singletons/Duets:

Other chart points:

ASPECTS & CONFIGURATIONS

THEMES & OTHER OBSERVATIONS

Equal Houses

Placidus Houses

Notes:

Born 12 November 1934, 16:40 EST (+5)
Cincinnati, Ohio, USA (39n10, 84w27)

Source: Birth certificate, copy on file (no forenames on the
certificate; another version posted online gives a full name,
but misspelt Moddox). Same data quoted in 'Contemporary
American Horoscopes'.
RR: AA   (Charles Milles Maddox)
       Data Collectors: Frank Clifford; Janice Mackay-Saunders

MARILYN MANSON

Singer, painter; self-proclaimed 'Antichrist Superstar'; cult
shock-rocker known for satanic persona; hits from 7/1994

Sun ....

Moon ....

Ascendant ....

     Chart Ruler ....

Fire ....

Earth ....

Air ....

Water ....

Cardinal ....

Fixed ....

Mutable ....

Mutual Reception: Sign emphasis:

Unaspected: House emphasis:

Retrograde: Singletons/Duets:

Other chart points:

Equal Houses

Placidus Houses

ASPECTS & CONFIGURATIONS

THEMES & OTHER OBSERVATIONS

Born 5 January 1969, 20:05 EST (+5)
Canton, Ohio, USA (40n48, 81w23)

Source: Birth certificate.

RR: AA   (Brian Hugh Warner)
                            Data Collector: Lois Rodden

Notes:

KARL MARX

Revolutionary philosopher, historian, political economist
and theorist; *The Communist Manifesto* pub. 21/2/1848

Sun ....

Moon ....

Ascendant ....

      Chart Ruler ....

Fire ....

Earth ....

Air ....

Water ....

Cardinal ....

Fixed ....

Mutable ....

Mutual Reception: Sign emphasis:

Unaspected: House emphasis:

Retrograde: Singletons/Duets:

Other chart points:

Equal Houses

Placidus Houses

ASPECTS & CONFIGURATIONS

THEMES & OTHER OBSERVATIONS

Born 5 May 1818, 02:00 LMT (-0:26:32)
Trier, Germany (49n45, 6e38)

Source: Birth certificate, and translation found in 'The
Portable Karl Marx' by Eugene Kamenka (Penguin, 1983), p.5,
copies on file. (LAT possible.)

RR: AA

(Carl Marx)
Data Collector: Sy Scholfield

Notes:

MATA HARI

Exotic dancer, courtesan, double agent, legendary *femme fatale*;
arrested 13/2/1917; executed by firing squad on 15/10/1917

Sun ....

Moon ....

Ascendant ....

      Chart Ruler ....

Fire ....

Earth ....

Air ....

Water ....

Cardinal ....

Fixed ....

Mutable ....

Mutual Reception: Sign emphasis:

Unaspected: House emphasis:

Retrograde: Singletons/Duets:

Other chart points:

Equal Houses

Placidus Houses

ASPECTS & CONFIGURATIONS

THEMES & OTHER OBSERVATIONS

Born 7 August 1876, 13:00 LMT (-0:23:04)
Leeuwarden, Netherlands (53n12, 5e46)

Source: Note from birth registry.

RR: AA

(Margaretha Geertruida Zelle)
Data Collector: Edwin Steinbrecher

Notes:

JOHN McENROE

Tennis champion, later an outspoken commentator; known for
petulant outbursts on court; #1 on-off from 3/3/1980-8/9/1985

Sun ....

Moon ....

Ascendant ....

     Chart Ruler ....

Fire ....

Earth ....

Air ....

Water ....

Cardinal ....

Fixed ....

Mutable ....

Mutual Reception: Sign emphasis:

Unaspected: House emphasis:

Retrograde: Singletons/Duets:

Other chart points:

Equal Houses

ASPECTS & CONFIGURATIONS

THEMES & OTHER OBSERVATIONS

Placidus Houses

Born 16 February 1959, 22:30 MET (-1)
Wiesbaden, Germany (50n05, 8e14)

Source: Biography 'McEnroe: A Rage for Perfection' by
Richard Evans (Simon and Schuster, 1982). Marc Penfield
quotes a letter from McEnroe's mother for 22:20.

RR: B   (John Patrick McEnroe, Jr)
          Data Collectors: Lois Rodden; Marc Penfield

Notes:

GILLIAN McKEITH

Holistic nutritionist; bossy, forceful TV host and best-selling
author of *You Are What You Eat* (pub. 17/6/2004; aired 29/6/2004)

Sun ....

Moon ....

Ascendant ....

      Chart Ruler ....

Fire ....

Earth ....

Air ....

Water ....

Cardinal ....

Fixed ....

Mutable ....

Mutual Reception: Sign emphasis:

Unaspected: House emphasis:

Retrograde: Singletons/Duets:

Other chart points:

Equal Houses

Placidus Houses

ASPECTS & CONFIGURATIONS

THEMES & OTHER OBSERVATIONS

Born 29 September 1959, 21:05 GDT (-1)
Perth, Scotland (56n24, 3w28)

Source: Birth certificate.

RR: AA

(Gillian McKeith)
Data Collector: Caroline Gerard

Notes:

MARILYN MONROE

Ultimate 20th-century sex symbol; childhood of abuse and
neglect; comedy actress typecast in 'dumb blonde' roles

Sun ....

Moon ....

Ascendant ....

     Chart Ruler ....

Fire ....

Earth ....

Air ....

Water ....

Cardinal ....

Fixed ....

Mutable ....

Mutual Reception: Sign emphasis:

Unaspected: House emphasis:

Retrograde: Singletons/Duets:

Other chart points:

Equal Houses

Placidus Houses

ASPECTS & CONFIGURATIONS

THEMES & OTHER OBSERVATIONS

Born 1 June 1926, 09:30 PST (+8)
Los Angeles, California, USA (34n03, 118w15)

Source: Birth certificate, copy on file.

RR: AA

(Norma Jeane Mortenson)
Data Collector: Bob Garner

Notes:

MICHAEL MOORE

Documentary filmmaker; liberal political commentator;
Bowling for Columbine (11/10/2002) and *Farenheit 9/11* (23/6/2004)

Sun ....

Moon ....

Ascendant ....

      Chart Ruler ....

Fire ....

Earth ....

Air ....

Water ....

Cardinal ....

Fixed ....

Mutable ....

Mutual Reception: Sign emphasis:

Unaspected: House emphasis:

Retrograde: Singletons/Duets:

Other chart points:

Equal Houses

Placidus Houses

ASPECTS & CONFIGURATIONS

THEMES & OTHER OBSERVATIONS

Born 23 April 1954, 12:45 EST (+5)
Flint, Michigan, USA (43n01, 83w41)

Source: Birth certificate quoted by Moore to Kasandra Green,
via Moore's sister Ann.

RR: AA

(Michael Francis Moore)
Data Collector: Edith Hathaway

Notes:

JIM MORRISON

Charismatic, explosive, quintessential rock star; singer, lyricist,
poet; unpredictable frontman of The Doors (formed 7/1965)

Sun ....

Moon ....

Ascendant ....

       Chart Ruler ....

Fire ....

Earth ....

Air ....

Water ....

Cardinal ....

Fixed ....

Mutable ....

Mutual Reception: Sign emphasis:

Unaspected: House emphasis:

Retrograde: Singletons/Duets:

Other chart points:

Equal Houses

Placidus Houses

ASPECTS & CONFIGURATIONS

THEMES & OTHER OBSERVATIONS

Born 8 December 1943, 11:55 EWT (+4)
Melbourne, Florida, USA (28n05, 80w36)

Source: Birth registration card, copy on file.

RR: AA

(James Douglas Morrison)
Data Collector: Bob Garner

Notes:

WOLFGANG AMADEUS MOZART

Highly influential composer of operas, sonatas and
symphonies; ambitious, prodigious musical maestro from age 5

Sun ....

Moon ....

Ascendant ....

      Chart Ruler ....

Fire ....

Earth ....

Air ....

Water ....

Cardinal ....

Fixed ....

Mutable ....

Mutual Reception: Sign emphasis:

Unaspected: House emphasis:

Retrograde: Singletons/Duets:

Other chart points:

Equal Houses

Placidus Houses

ASPECTS & CONFIGURATIONS

THEMES & OTHER OBSERVATIONS

Born 27 January 1756, 20:00 LAT (-0:38:51)
Salzburg, Austria (47n48, 13e02)

Source: Baptismal certificate, copy on file. Same in his
father's letter, as quoted in a biography by Jacques Gabriel
Prod'homme. (LAT, not LMT, was in use.)

RR: AA   (Joannes Chrysostomus Wolfgangus Theophilus Mozart)
                    Data Collectors: Lois Rodden; Sy Scholfield

Notes:

BENITO MUSSOLINI

Il Duce; Fascist dictator; Prime Minister of Italy (31/10/1922–
25/7/1943); led Italy into World War II on 10/6/1940

Sun ....

Moon ....

Ascendant ....

     Chart Ruler ....

Fire ....

Earth ....

Air ....

Water ....

Cardinal ....

Fixed ....

Mutable ....

Mutual Reception: Sign emphasis:

Unaspected: House emphasis:

Retrograde: Singletons/Duets:

Other chart points:

Equal Houses

Placidus Houses

ASPECTS & CONFIGURATIONS

THEMES & OTHER OBSERVATIONS

Born 29 July 1883, 14:00 LMT (Rome Time -0:49:56)
Dovia di Predappio, Italy (44n06 11e58)

Source: Birth certificate, copy on file.

RR: AA   (Benito Mussolini)
Data Collectors: M. and F. Gauquelin; Sy Scholfield

Notes:

MARTINA NAVRATILOVA

Outstanding singles and doubles tennis champion; 59 Grand
Slam titles (1974-2006); gay rights advocate; defected 9/1975

Sun ....

Moon ....

Ascendant ....

      Chart Ruler ....

Fire ....

Earth ....

Air ....

Water ....

Cardinal ....

Fixed ....

Mutable ....

Mutual Reception: Sign emphasis:

Unaspected: House emphasis:

Retrograde: Singletons/Duets:

Other chart points:

Equal Houses

Placidus Houses

ASPECTS & CONFIGURATIONS

THEMES & OTHER OBSERVATIONS

Born 18 October 1956, 16:40 MET (-1)
Prague, Czechoslovakia (50n05, 14e26)

Source: From her to Frank Clifford, 1995 ('16:40 give or
take a few minutes').

RR: A   (Martina Subertova)
                    Data Collector: Frank Clifford

Notes:

DENNIS NILSEN

Serial killer; former Job Centre worker; seduced and killed
15 men and boys (30/12/1978–26/1/1983); sentenced 4/11/1983

Sun ....

Moon ....

Ascendant ....

     Chart Ruler ....

Fire ....

Earth ....

Air ....

Water ....

Cardinal ....

Fixed ....

Mutable ....

Mutual Reception: Sign emphasis:

Unaspected: House emphasis:

Retrograde: Singletons/Duets:

Other chart points:

Equal Houses

Placidus Houses

ASPECTS & CONFIGURATIONS

THEMES & OTHER OBSERVATIONS

Born 23 November 1945, 04:00 GMT (+0)
Fraserburgh, Scotland (57n42, 2w00)

Source: Birth certificate.

RR: AA   (Dennis Andrew Nilsen)
Data Collector: Paul Wright

Notes:

ANAÏS NIN

Writer of erotica; feminist diarist given mythological status,
famous for her insightful, intimate journals (1931–1974)

Sun ....

Moon ....

Ascendant ....

      Chart Ruler ....

Fire ....

Earth ....

Air ....

Water ....

Cardinal ....

Fixed ....

Mutable ....

Mutual Reception: Sign emphasis:

Unaspected: House emphasis:

Retrograde: Singletons/Duets:

Other chart points:

Equal Houses

Placidus Houses

ASPECTS & CONFIGURATIONS

THEMES & OTHER OBSERVATIONS

Born 21 February 1903, 20:25 LMT (Paris Time 0:09:20)
Paris, France (48n52, 2e20)

Source: Birth certificate.

RR: AA   (Angela Anaïs Juana Antolina Rosa Edelmira Nin)
Data Collector: Jany Bessiere

Notes:

RICHARD NIXON

Disgraced US President (20/1/1969 to 9/8/1974); Congress 2/1/1947
to 1/12/1950, Senate to 1/1/1953; Watergate break-in 17/6/1972

Sun ....

Moon ....

Ascendant ....

    Chart Ruler ....

Fire ....

Earth ....

Air ....

Water ....

Cardinal ....

Fixed ....

Mutable ....

Mutual Reception: Sign emphasis:

Unaspected: House emphasis:

Retrograde: Singletons/Duets:

Other chart points:

Equal Houses

Placidus Houses

ASPECTS & CONFIGURATIONS

THEMES & OTHER OBSERVATIONS

Born 9 January 1913, 21:35 PST (+8)
Yorba Linda, California, USA (33n53, 117w49)
Source: Birth certificate. (Born at home; confirmed by a Nixon
Library archivist to Pat Taglilatelo, 11/2008.) (His wife
Pat was born Thelma Catharine Ryan on 16 March 1912, 03:25
PST, Ely, Nevada, USA (39n15, 114w53). Birth certificate
quoted by Nevada State Library and Archives online.)
RR: AA   (Richard Milhous Nixon)
Data Collector: T. Pat Davis; Pat Taglilatelo

Notes:

BARACK OBAMA

Won Democratic nomination 3/6/2008 and US Presidential
Election campaign 4/11/2008; elected to Senate 11/2004

Sun ....

Moon ....

Ascendant ....

     Chart Ruler ....

Fire ....

Earth ....

Air ....

Water ....

Cardinal ....

Fixed ....

Mutable ....

Mutual Reception: Sign emphasis:

Unaspected: House emphasis:

Retrograde: Singletons/Duets:

Other chart points:

Equal Houses

Placidus Houses

ASPECTS & CONFIGURATIONS

THEMES & OTHER OBSERVATIONS

Born 4 August 1961, 19:24 AHST (+10)
Honolulu, Oahu, Hawaii, USA (21n18, 157w52)

Source: Birth certificate posted on Obama's website, copy on
file.

RR: AA   (Barack Hussein Obama II)
           Data Collector: Various astrologers

Notes:

LEE HARVEY OSWALD

Alleged lone assassin of JFK (qv) 22/11/1963; disturbed child
fantasist; former Marine; defected to USSR 10/1959–1/6/1962

Sun ....

Moon ....

Ascendant ....

      Chart Ruler ....

Fire ....

Earth ....

Air ....

Water ....

Cardinal ....

Fixed ....

Mutable ....

Mutual Reception: Sign emphasis:

Unaspected: House emphasis:

Retrograde: Singletons/Duets:

Other chart points:

Equal Houses

Placidus Houses

ASPECTS & CONFIGURATIONS

THEMES & OTHER OBSERVATIONS

Born 18 October 1939, 21:55 CST (+6)
New Orleans, Louisiana, USA (29n57, 90w05)

Source: From Oswald's mother to T. Pat Davis.

RR: A

(Lee Harvey Oswald)
Data Collector: T. Pat Davis

Notes:

EMMELINE PANKHURST

Militant leader of the British suffragettes; first group founded
on 25/7/1889, Women's Social and Political Union on 10/10/1903

Sun ....

Moon ....

Ascendant ....

      Chart Ruler ....

Fire ....

Earth ....

Air ....

Water ....

Cardinal ....

Fixed ....

Mutable ....

Mutual Reception: Sign emphasis:

Unaspected: House emphasis:

Retrograde: Singletons/Duets:

Other chart points:

Equal Houses

Placidus Houses

ASPECTS & CONFIGURATIONS

THEMES & OTHER OBSERVATIONS

Born 15 July 1858, 21:30 GMT (+0)
Manchester, England (53n30, 2w15)

Source: Time from her to Edward Lyndoe. Pankhurst gave the
date 14 July, the day of the storming of the Bastille; her
birth certificate gives 15 July.

RR: A
                    (Emiline Goulden)
Data Collector: Edward Lyndoe

Notes:

CAMILLA PARKER BOWLES

Wife of Prince Charles (from 9/4/2005); their extra-marital affair
was exposed in 6/1992; leaked 'Camillagate' recordings 13/11/1992

Sun ....

Moon ....

Ascendant ....

      Chart Ruler ....

Fire ....

Earth ....

Air ....

Water ....

Cardinal ....

Fixed ....

Mutable ....

Mutual Reception: Sign emphasis:

Unaspected: House emphasis:

Retrograde: Singletons/Duets:

Other chart points:

Equal Houses

Placidus Houses

ASPECTS & CONFIGURATIONS

THEMES & OTHER OBSERVATIONS

Born 17 July 1947, 07:00 DGWT (-2)
Denmark Hill, London, England (51n28, 0w06)

Source: From the biography 'Camilla: The King's Mistress' by
Caroline Graham (HarperTorch, 1995), p.1.

RR: B   (Camilla Rosemary Shand)
          Data Collectors: Frank Clifford; Sy Scholfield

Notes:

DOLLY PARTON

Flamboyant Country singer-songwriter-musician; actress; first
hit in 1/1967; mainstream commercial hits from 1/1978

Sun ....

Moon ....

Ascendant ....

     Chart Ruler ....

Fire ....

Earth ....

Air ....

Water ....

Cardinal ....

Fixed ....

Mutable ....

Equal Houses

Mutual Reception: Sign emphasis:

Unaspected: House emphasis:

Retrograde: Singletons/Duets:

Other chart points:

ASPECTS & CONFIGURATIONS

THEMES & OTHER OBSERVATIONS

Placidus Houses

Born 19 January 1946, 20:25 CST (+6)
Little Pigeon River, Sevierville, Tennessee, USA
(35n52, 83w34)

Source: Note from birth registry, copy on file.

RR: AA

(Dolly Rebecca Parton)
Data Collector: Frank Clifford

Notes:

PABLO PICASSO

Legendary, prolific Expressionist painter and sculptor; co-created Cubism; complex, powerful avant-garde works of art

Sun ....

Moon ....

Ascendant ....

      Chart Ruler ....

Fire ....

Earth ....

Air ....

Water ....

Cardinal ....

Fixed ....

Mutable ....

Mutual Reception: Sign emphasis:

Unaspected: House emphasis:

Retrograde: Singletons/Duets:

Other chart points:

Equal Houses

Placidus Houses

ASPECTS & CONFIGURATIONS

THEMES & OTHER OBSERVATIONS

Born 25 October 1881, 23:15 LMT (Madrid Time +0:14:44)
Malaga, Spain (36n43, 4w25)

Source: Birth certificate.

RR: AA   (Pablo Diego Jose Francisco Picasso)
      Data Collector: Filipe Ferreira

Notes:

BRAD PITT

Actor; sex symbol from 5/1991; married Jennifer Aniston
29/7/2000 (split 1/2005); relationship with Angelina Jolie (qv)

Sun ....

Moon ....

Ascendant ....

　　　　Chart Ruler ....

Fire ....

Earth ....

Air ....

Water ....

Cardinal ....

Fixed ....

Mutable ....

Mutual Reception: 　　　　Sign emphasis:

Unaspected: 　　　　　　　House emphasis:

Retrograde: 　　　　　　　Singletons/Duets:

Other chart points:

Equal Houses

Placidus Houses

ASPECTS & CONFIGURATIONS

THEMES & OTHER OBSERVATIONS

Born 18 December 1963, 06:31 CST (+6)
Shawnee, Oklahoma, USA (35n20, 96w56)

Source: From Pitt to a trusted colleague of Lois Rodden.
(Ex-wife Jennifer Aniston was born on 11 February 1969,
22:22 PST, Hollywood, California, USA (34n06, 118w20). Birth
certificate quoted by Marc Penfield and Sue Jorgenson.)
RR: A 　　　　　　　　　　　　　(William Bradley Pitt)
　　　　　　　　　　　　　Data Collector: Lois Rodden

Notes:

SYLVIA PLATH

Confessional poet, novelist, short story writer; her novel
The Bell Jar pub. 1963; married Ted Hughes 16/6/1956

Sun ....

Moon ....

Ascendant ....

     Chart Ruler ....

Fire ....

Earth ....

Air ....

Water ....

Cardinal ....

Fixed ....

Mutable ....

Mutual Reception: Sign emphasis:

Unaspected: House emphasis:

Retrograde: Singletons/Duets:

Other chart points:

Equal Houses

Placidus Houses

ASPECTS & CONFIGURATIONS

THEMES & OTHER OBSERVATIONS

Born 27 October 1932, 14:10 EST (+5)
Jamaica Plain, Boston, Massachusetts, USA (42n19, 71w07)

Source: From her mother, as quoted by Ruth Hale Oliver.

RR: A   (Sylvia Plath)
Data Collector: Ruth Hale Oliver

Notes:

ELVIS PRESLEY

'The King'; iconic, photogenic entertainer; commercial
breakthrough in 2/1956; generous, voyeuristic, gluttonous

Sun ....

Moon ....

Ascendant ....

      Chart Ruler ....

Fire ....

Earth ....

Air ....

Water ....

Cardinal ....

Fixed ....

Mutable ....

Mutual Reception: Sign emphasis:

Unaspected: House emphasis:

Retrograde: Singletons/Duets:

Other chart points:

Equal Houses

Placidus Houses

ASPECTS & CONFIGURATIONS

THEMES & OTHER OBSERVATIONS

Born 8 January 1935, 04:35 CST (+6)
Tupelo, Mississippi, USA (34n15, 88w42)

Source: Birth certificate, copy on file (another version,
without a birth time, lists his middle name as 'Aron').

RR: AA

(Elvis Aaron Presley)
Data Collector: Eugene Moore

Notes:

JonBenét Ramsey

Child beauty pageant contestant; victim of an infamous,
unsolved murder (26/12/1996); mother died of cancer 24/6/2006

Sun ....

Moon ....

Ascendant ....

     Chart Ruler ....

Fire ....

Earth ....

Air ....

Water ....

Cardinal ....

Fixed ....

Mutable ....

Mutual Reception: Sign emphasis:

Unaspected: House emphasis:

Retrograde: Singletons/Duets:

Other chart points:

Equal Houses

Placidus Houses

ASPECTS & CONFIGURATIONS

THEMES & OTHER OBSERVATIONS

Notes:

Born 6 August 1990, 01:36 EDT (+4)
Atlanta, Georgia, USA (33n45, 84w23)

Source: Birth announcement, as seen on 'Larry King Live'
(12/11/02). Same details in 'The Death of Innocence' by John
Ramsey, Patsy Ramsey and Patricia Ann Ramsey (Thomas Nelson,
Nashville, 2000).
RR: AA
     (JonBenét Patricia Ramsey)
     Data Collector: Frank Clifford

NANCY REAGAN

First Lady of California (3/1/1967 to 7/1/1975) and later the
USA (20/1/1981 to 20/1/1989); met Ronald Reagan 15/11/1949

Sun ....

Moon ....

Ascendant ....

       Chart Ruler ....

Fire ....

Earth ....

Air ....

Water ....

Cardinal ....

Fixed ....

Mutable ....

Mutual Reception: Sign emphasis:

Unaspected: House emphasis:

Retrograde: Singletons/Duets:

Other chart points:

Equal Houses

Placidus Houses

ASPECTS & CONFIGURATIONS

THEMES & OTHER OBSERVATIONS

Born 6 July 1921, 13:18 EDT (+4)
Manhattan, New York, USA (40n46, 73w59)
Source: Birth certificate (without time) printed in 'Nancy
Reagan: the Unauthorized Biography' by Kitty Kelley (Simon
& Schuster, 1991); time from 'Fly Away Home' by John Weld,
p.187 (his mother Deborah Lewis cast a horoscope for a 17-
year-old Nancy). Copies of both on file.
RR: B
          (Anne Frances Robbins)
          Data Collector: David Stenn

Notes:

ANTHONY ROBBINS

Celebrity motivational and NLP speaker-writer; *Personal Power*
programme; authoured *Awaken the Giant Within* (9/1992)

Sun ....

Moon ....

Ascendant ....

      Chart Ruler ....

Fire ....

Earth ....

Air ....

Water ....

Cardinal ....

Fixed ....

Mutable ....

Mutual Reception: Sign emphasis:

Unaspected: House emphasis:

Retrograde: Singletons/Duets:

Other chart points:

Equal Houses

Placidus Houses

ASPECTS & CONFIGURATIONS

THEMES & OTHER OBSERVATIONS

Born 29 February 1960, 20:10 PST (+8)
Los Angeles, California, USA (34n03, 118w15)

Source: Birth certificate, copy on file.

RR: AA

(Anthony John Mohorovick)
Data Collector: Frank Clifford

Notes:

GENE RODDENBERRY

Screenwriter, producer; creator of the (part adventure story,
part morality parable) cult TV show *Star Trek* (prem. 8/9/1966)

Sun ....

Moon ....

Ascendant ....

      Chart Ruler ....

Fire ....

Earth ....

Air ....

Water ....

Cardinal ....

Fixed ....

Mutable ....

Mutual Reception: Sign emphasis:

Unaspected: House emphasis:

Retrograde: Singletons/Duets:

Other chart points:

Equal Houses

Placidus Houses

ASPECTS & CONFIGURATIONS

THEMES & OTHER OBSERVATIONS

Born 19 August 1921, 01:35 MST (+7)
El Paso, Texas, USA (31n45, 106w29)

Source: Birth certificate.

RR: AA

(Eugene Wesley Roddenberry)
Data Collector: Jim Eshelman

Notes:

ANITA RODDICK

Entrepreneur, activist; founder of The Body Shop on 26/3/1976,
based on ethical, fair trade consumerism (sold it on 17/3/2006)

Sun ....

Moon ....

Ascendant ....

      Chart Ruler ....

Fire ....

Earth ....

Air ....

Water ....

Cardinal ....

Fixed ....

Mutable ....

Mutual Reception: Sign emphasis:

Unaspected: House emphasis:

Retrograde: Singletons/Duets:

Other chart points:

Equal Houses

Placidus Houses

ASPECTS & CONFIGURATIONS

THEMES & OTHER OBSERVATIONS

Born 23 October 1942, 12:50 GDT (−1)
Littlehampton, England (50n48, 0w33)

Source: Roddick, via her PA, to her astrologer (given as
'1pm'; when asked for a more exact time, the astrologer was
told 'perhaps ten minutes to 1pm'). (Sy Scholfield quotes the
birth registry for her birth name.)
RR: A
                     (Anita Lucia Perella)
                Data Collector: Frank Clifford

Notes:

ELEANOR ROOSEVELT

US First Lady (4/3/1933–12/4/1945); UN Delegate from 31/12/1946; approved Universal Decl. of Human Rights 10/12/1948

Sun ....

Moon ....

Ascendant ....

      Chart Ruler ....

Fire ....

Earth ....

Air ....

Water ....

Cardinal ....

Fixed ....

Mutable ....

Mutual Reception: Sign emphasis:

Unaspected: House emphasis:

Retrograde: Singletons/Duets:

Other chart points:

Equal Houses

Placidus Houses

ASPECTS & CONFIGURATIONS

THEMES & OTHER OBSERVATIONS

Born 11 October 1884, 11:00 EST (+5)
New York, New York, USA (40n43, 74w00)

Source: Family register, printed in 'The Eleanor Roosevelt Story' by Archibald Macleish, (Houghton Mifflin, 1965), p.2, copy on file.

RR: AA   (Anna Eleanor Roosevelt)
Data Collector: Joan Negus

Notes:

DIANA ROSS

Glamorous, pioneering singer; actress; fame from 6/1964
with Motown girl group The Supremes; solo from 1/1970

Sun ....

Moon ....

Ascendant ....

     Chart Ruler ....

Fire ....

Earth ....

Air ....

Water ....

Cardinal ....

Fixed ....

Mutable ....

Mutual Reception: Sign emphasis:

Unaspected: House emphasis:

Retrograde: Singletons/Duets:

Other chart points:

ASPECTS & CONFIGURATIONS

THEMES & OTHER OBSERVATIONS

Equal Houses

Placidus Houses

Born 26 March 1944, 23:46 EWT (+4)
Detroit, Michigan, USA (42n20, 83w03)

Source: Birth certificate quoted in 'Contemporary American
Horoscopes' and 'The Gauquelin Book of American Charts'.
('Diana' typed on certificate; known as 'Diane' to family.)

RR: AA   (Diana Ernestine Ross)
Data Collectors: Janice Mackay-Saunders; M. and F. Gauquelin

Notes:

SALMAN RUSHDIE

Novelist; fame from second novel *Midnight's Children* (4/1981);
The Satanic Verses (pub. 9/1988) led to a *fatwa* (issued 14/2/1989)

Sun ....

Moon ....

Ascendant ....

      Chart Ruler ....

Fire ....

Earth ....

Air ....

Water ....

Cardinal ....

Fixed ....

Mutable ....

Mutual Reception: Sign emphasis:

Unaspected: House emphasis:

Retrograde: Singletons/Duets:

Other chart points:

Equal Houses

Placidus Houses

ASPECTS & CONFIGURATIONS

THEMES & OTHER OBSERVATIONS

Born 19 June 1947, 02:30 IST (-5.30)
Bombay (now Mumbai), India (18n58, 72e50)

Source: From Rushdie to Penny Allen (former wife of novelist
Ian McEwan), who told astrologer Catriona Mundle; copy of
Mundle's letter to Sally Davis on file.

RR: A   (Ahmed Salman Rushdie)
      Data Collector: Catriona Mundle

Notes:

BERTRAND RUSSELL

Prolific writer; liberal activist; known for work in mathematical
logic (Russell's Paradox, spring 1901) and analytic philosophy

Sun ....

Moon ....

Ascendant ....

     Chart Ruler ....

Fire ....

Earth ....

Air ....

Water ....

Cardinal ....

Fixed ....

Mutable ....

Mutual Reception: Sign emphasis:

Unaspected: House emphasis:

Retrograde: Singletons/Duets:

Other chart points:

Equal Houses

Placidus Houses

ASPECTS & CONFIGURATIONS

THEMES & OTHER OBSERVATIONS

Born 18 May 1872, 17:45 GMT (+0)
Trellech, Wales (51n45, 2w43)

Source: Biography 'The Life of Bertrand Russell' by Ronald
W. Clark (Jonathan Cape and Weidenfeld & Nicolson, 1975),
p.23, copy on file. Same in 'Bertrand Russell the Passionate
Sceptic: A Biography' by Alan Wood (Allen & Unwin, 1957),
p. 15.
RR: B   (Bertrand Arthur William Russell)
                    Data Collectors: Frank Clifford; Sy Scholfield

Notes:

MARQUIS DE SADE

Licentious, libertine, revolutionary aristocrat and author of
sadomasochistic novels; major scandal 3/4/1768 led to prison

Sun ....

Moon ....

Ascendant ....

      Chart Ruler ....

Fire ....

Earth ....

Air ....

Water ....

Cardinal ....

Fixed ....

Mutable ....

Mutual Reception: Sign emphasis:

Unaspected: House emphasis:

Retrograde: Singletons/Duets:

Other chart points:

Equal Houses

Placidus Houses

ASPECTS & CONFIGURATIONS

THEMES & OTHER OBSERVATIONS

Born 2 June 1740, 17:00 LAT (-0:11:50)
Paris, France (48n52, 2e20)

Source: Birth record. (LAT not LMT in use.)

RR: AA   (Donatien Alphonse François, Comte de Sade)
                 Data Collector: Richard Rongier

Notes:

ARNOLD SCHWARZENEGGER

Bodybuilder (titles from 1966); actor (success in *The Terminator*,
rel. 26/10/1984); Governor of California from 7/10/2003

Sun ....

Moon ....

Ascendant ....

      Chart Ruler ....

Fire ....

Earth ....

Air ....

Water ....

Cardinal ....

Fixed ....

Mutable ....

Mutual Reception: Sign emphasis:

Unaspected: House emphasis:

Retrograde: Singletons/Duets:

Other chart points:

Equal Houses

Placidus Houses

ASPECTS & CONFIGURATIONS

THEMES & OTHER OBSERVATIONS

Born 30 July 1947, 04:10 MEDT (-2)
Graz, Austria (47n05, 15e27)

Source: From him to a colleague of Doris Chase Doane. (Thal,
a suburb of Graz, is sometimes given as his birth place.)

RR: A

(Arnold Alois Schwarzenegger)
Data Collector: Doris Chase Doane

Notes:

George Bernard Shaw

Socialist playwright, dramatist and satirist who addressed
hypocrisy and the indignities of capitalism, war and poverty

Sun ....

Moon ....

Ascendant ....

      Chart Ruler ....

Fire ....

Earth ....

Air ....

Water ....

Cardinal ....

Fixed ....

Mutable ....

Mutual Reception: Sign emphasis:

Unaspected: House emphasis:

Retrograde: Singletons/Duets:

Other chart points:

Equal Houses

Placidus Houses

ASPECTS & CONFIGURATIONS

THEMES & OTHER OBSERVATIONS

Born 26 July 1856, 00:55 LMT (+0:25:00)
Dublin, Ireland (53n20, 6w15)

Source: Family Bible.

RR: AA

(George Bernard Shaw)
Data Collector: Mary K. Greer

Notes:

MARY SHELLEY

Novelist, short story writer and dramatist; best known for
the Gothic novel *Frankenstein* (pub. 1/1818); tragic life

Sun ....

Moon ....

Ascendant ....

      Chart Ruler ....

Fire ....

Earth ....

Air ....

Water ....

Cardinal ....

Fixed ....

Mutable ....

Mutual Reception: Sign emphasis:

Unaspected: House emphasis:

Retrograde: Singletons/Duets:

Other chart points:

Equal Houses

Placidus Houses

ASPECTS & CONFIGURATIONS

THEMES & OTHER OBSERVATIONS

Born 30 August 1797, 23:20 LMT (+0:00:28)
Somers Town, London, England (51n32, 0w08)

Source: Father's journal, copy on file.

RR: AA

(Mary Wollstonecraft Godwin)
Data Collector: Barbara Lynne Devlin

Notes:

PERCY BYSSHE SHELLEY

Visionary, Romantic poet and uncompromising idealist;
eloped with Mary Shelley (qv) on 28/7/1814; drowned 8/7/1822

Sun ....

Moon ....

Ascendant ....

       Chart Ruler ....

Fire ....

Earth ....

Air ....

Water ....

Cardinal ....

Fixed ....

Mutable ....

Mutual Reception: Sign emphasis:

Unaspected: House emphasis:

Retrograde: Singletons/Duets:

Other chart points:

Equal Houses

Placidus Houses

ASPECTS & CONFIGURATIONS

THEMES & OTHER OBSERVATIONS

Born 4 August 1792, 22:00 LMT (+0:01:24)
Horsham, England (51n04, 0w21)

Source: Family Bible (transcription viewed by Sy Scholfield).
Same data from his father and grandfather quoted in
'Shelley: A Biography' by Jean Overton Fuller (1968). (LAT
is possible: +0:06:57)
RR: AA
                              (Percy Bysshe Shelley)
           Data Collectors: Sy Scholfield; Stephen Erlewine

Notes:

BETTY SHINE

Spiritual healer, influential medium and author of a series of
'Mind' books from 1/1990; former opera singer and palmist

Sun ....

Moon ....

Ascendant ....

      Chart Ruler ....

Fire ....

Earth ....

Air ....

Water ....

Cardinal ....

Fixed ....

Mutable ....

Mutual Reception: Sign emphasis:

Unaspected: House emphasis:

Retrograde: Singletons/Duets:

Other chart points:

Equal Houses

Placidus Houses

ASPECTS & CONFIGURATIONS

THEMES & OTHER OBSERVATIONS

8 March 1929, 08:15 GMT (+0)
Kennington, London, England (51n29, 0w07)

Source: Shine to Mike Zitaglio; chart printed in his ebook
'Passages', copy on file.

RR: A

(Betty Alice Davis)
Data Collector: Frank Clifford

Notes:

DON SIMPSON

Film producer (*Flashdance*, 4/1983, *Beverly Hills Cop*, 12/1984
and *Top Gun*, 5/1986); excessive, decadent, S&M, drug lifestyle

Sun ....

Moon ....

Ascendant ....

     Chart Ruler ....

Fire ....

Earth ....

Air ....

Water ....

Cardinal ....

Fixed ....

Mutable ....

Mutual Reception: Sign emphasis:

Unaspected: House emphasis:

Retrograde: Singletons/Duets:

Other chart points:

Equal Houses

Placidus Houses

ASPECTS & CONFIGURATIONS

THEMES & OTHER OBSERVATIONS

Born 29 October 1943, 10:53 PWT (+7)
Seattle, Washington, USA (47n36, 122w20)

Source: Birth certificate, copy on file.

RR: AA   (Donald Clarence Simpson)
     Data Collector: Frank Clifford

Notes:

O.J. SIMPSON

American football hero (1969–79); actor; accused of murder
6/1994; acquitted 3/10/1995; found guilty of robbery 3/10/2008

Sun ....

Moon ....

Ascendant ....

     Chart Ruler ....

Fire ....

Earth ....

Air ....

Water ....

Cardinal ....

Fixed ....

Mutable ....

Mutual Reception: Sign emphasis:

Unaspected: House emphasis:

Retrograde: Singletons/Duets:

Other chart points:

Equal Houses

Placidus Houses

ASPECTS & CONFIGURATIONS

THEMES & OTHER OBSERVATIONS

Notes:

Born 9 July 1947, 08:08 PST (+8)
San Francisco, California, USA (37n47, 122w25)

Source: Birth certificate quoted in 'Contemporary American Horoscopes'. (Ex-wife Nicole Brown was born 19 May 1959, 02:00 MET (-1), Frankfurt am Main, Germany (50n07, 8e40). Birth certificate from Monika Gerber.)
RR: AA   (Orenthal James Simpson)
Data Collector: Janice Mackay-Saunders

FRANK SINATRA

Iconic, era-defining swing singer from 1941; 'Rat Pack'
entertainer; actor; alleged links with organized crime figures

Sun ....

Moon ....

Ascendant ....

    Chart Ruler ....

Fire ....

Earth ....

Air ....

Water ....

Cardinal ....

Fixed ....

Mutable ....

Mutual Reception: Sign emphasis:

Unaspected: House emphasis:

Retrograde: Singletons/Duets:

Other chart points:

Equal Houses

Placidus Houses

ASPECTS & CONFIGURATIONS

THEMES & OTHER OBSERVATIONS

Born 12 December 1915, 03:00 EST (+5)
Hoboken, New Jersey, USA (40n45, 74w02)

Source: From his father to Lynne Palmer.

RR: A

(Francis Albert Sinatra)
Data Collector: Lynne Palmer

Notes:

BRITNEY SPEARS

Singer; former child star (1992–3); chart success from 11/1998
with ...*Baby One More Time*; publicized meltdown from 2/2007

Sun ....

Moon ....

Ascendant ....

      Chart Ruler ....

Fire ....

Earth ....

Air ....

Water ....

Cardinal ....

Fixed ....

Mutable ....

Mutual Reception: Sign emphasis:

Unaspected: House emphasis:

Retrograde: Singletons/Duets:

Other chart points:

Equal Houses

Placidus Houses

ASPECTS & CONFIGURATIONS

THEMES & OTHER OBSERVATIONS

Born 2 December 1981, 01:30 CST (+6)
McComb, Mississippi, USA (31n15, 90w27)

Source: From her and her mother to Barry Street of The
Astrology Shop, 78 Neal Street, Covent Garden, London in
November 2000.

RR: A

(Britney Jean Spears)
Data Collector: Barry Street

Notes:

AARON SPELLING

Wealthy, prolific TV producer of *The Love Boat*, *Charlie's Angels*,
Dynasty, *Starsky and Hutch*, *Beverly Hills 90210*, *Charmed*

Sun ....

Moon ....

Ascendant ....

      Chart Ruler ....

Fire ....

Earth ....

Air ....

Water ....

Cardinal ....

Fixed ....

Mutable ....

Mutual Reception: Sign emphasis:

Unaspected: House emphasis:

Retrograde: Singletons/Duets:

Other chart points:

Equal Houses

Placidus Houses

ASPECTS & CONFIGURATIONS

THEMES & OTHER OBSERVATIONS

Born 22 April 1923, 12:30 CST (+6)
Dallas, Texas, USA (32n47, 96w48)

Source: Birth certificate, copy on file (no name on the
original certificate).

RR: AA

(Aaron Spelling)
Data Collector: Frank Clifford

Notes:

STEVEN SPIELBERG

Record-breaking, influential producer-director of *Jaws* (6/1975),
E.T. (6/1982), *Jurassic Park* (6/1993), *Schindler's List* (12/1993)

Sun ....

Moon ....

Ascendant ....

    Chart Ruler ....

Fire ....

Earth ....

Air ....

Water ....

Cardinal ....

Fixed ....

Mutable ....

Mutual Reception: Sign emphasis:

Unaspected: House emphasis:

Retrograde: Singletons/Duets:

Other chart points:

Equal Houses

Placidus Houses

ASPECTS & CONFIGURATIONS

THEMES & OTHER OBSERVATIONS

Born 18 December 1946, 18:16 EST (+5)
Cincinnati, Ohio, USA (39n10, 84w27)

Source: Birth certificate, copy on file; same in 'Contemporary American Horoscopes'.

RR: AA   (Steven Allan Spielberg)
    Data Collectors: Linda Lineauveuer; Janice Mackay-Saunders

Notes:

SYLVESTER STALLONE

Actor, director, producer, screenwriter; macho, heroic leads in
the *Rocky* (from 11/1976) and *Rambo* (from 10/1982) film series

Sun ....

Moon ....

Ascendant ....

     Chart Ruler ....

Fire ....

Earth ....

Air ....

Water ....

Cardinal ....

Fixed ....

Mutable ....

Mutual Reception: Sign emphasis:

Unaspected: House emphasis:

Retrograde: Singletons/Duets:

Other chart points:

Equal Houses

Placidus Houses

ASPECTS & CONFIGURATIONS

THEMES & OTHER OBSERVATIONS

Born 6 July 1946, 19:20 EDT (+4)
Manhattan, New York, USA (40n46, 73w59)

Source: From his astrologer-mother, as quoted by Jany
Bessiere.

RR: A   (Sylvester Gardenzio Stallone; other sources add
          Michael as his first name)
          Data Collector: Jany Bessiere

Notes:

ROBERT LOUIS STEVENSON

Novelist, poet, travel writer; writing themes of intrigue and
buccaneering; *Treasure Island* serialized from 10/1881; sickly

Sun ....

Moon ....

Ascendant ....

      Chart Ruler ....

Fire ....

Earth ....

Air ....

Water ....

Cardinal ....

Fixed ....

Mutable ....

Mutual Reception: Sign emphasis:

Unaspected: House emphasis:

Retrograde: Singletons/Duets:

Other chart points:

Equal Houses

Placidus Houses

ASPECTS & CONFIGURATIONS

THEMES & OTHER OBSERVATIONS

Born 13 November 1850, 13:30 GMT (+0)
Edinburgh, Scotland (55n57, 3w13)

Source: Baby book, published as 'Stevenson's Baby Book:
Being the Record of the Sayings and Doings of Robert Louis
Balfour Stevenson' (John Henry Nash & John Howell, 1922).
(Copy of birth record, without a birth time, on file.)
RR: AA   (Robert Lewis Balfour Stevenson)
                     Data Collector: Sy Scholfied

Notes:

MARTHA STEWART

Multimedia magnate; TV host; publisher; authored books on
cookery, homemaking, gracious living; high-flying perfectionist

Sun ....

Moon ....

Ascendant ....

    Chart Ruler ....

Fire ....

Earth ....

Air ....

Water ....

Cardinal ....

Fixed ....

Mutable ....

Mutual Reception: Sign emphasis:

Unaspected: House emphasis:

Retrograde: Singletons/Duets:

Other chart points:

Equal Houses

Placidus Houses

ASPECTS & CONFIGURATIONS

THEMES & OTHER OBSERVATIONS

Born 3 August 1941, 13:33 EDT (+4)
Jersey City, New Jersey, USA (40n44, 74w05)

Source: Birth certificate, copy on file.

RR: AA

(Martha Kostyra)
Data Collector: Lois Rodden

Notes:

MARIE STOPES

Family planning pioneer (clinic from 17/3/1921); influential sex
manual *Married Love* pub. 3/1918; attacked by Catholic Church

Sun ....

Moon ....

Ascendant ....

     Chart Ruler ....

Fire ....

Earth ....

Air ....

Water ....

Cardinal ....

Fixed ....

Mutable ....

Mutual Reception: Sign emphasis:

Unaspected: House emphasis:

Retrograde: Singletons/Duets:

Other chart points:

Equal Houses

Placidus Houses

ASPECTS & CONFIGURATIONS

THEMES & OTHER OBSERVATIONS

Born 15 October 1880, 04:10 GMT (+0)
Edinburgh, Scotland (55n57, 3w13)

Source: Birth certificate, copy on file.

RR: AA   (Marie-Charlotte Carmichael Stopes)
Data Collector: Frank Clifford

Notes:

BARBRA STREISAND

Iconic award-winning singer-songwriter; film and theatre
actress; stardom from 3/1962; controlling perfectionist

Sun ....

Moon ....

Ascendant ....

    Chart Ruler ....

Fire ....

Earth ....

Air ....

Water ....

Cardinal ....

Fixed ....

Mutable ....

Mutual Reception: Sign emphasis:

Unaspected: House emphasis:

Retrograde: Singletons/Duets:

Other chart points:

ASPECTS & CONFIGURATIONS

THEMES & OTHER OBSERVATIONS

Equal Houses

Placidus Houses

Born 24 April 1942, 05:04 EWT (+4)
Brooklyn, New York, USA (40n38, 73w56)

Source: Birth announcement, as printed in a biography. Edwin
Steinbrecher quotes Streisand to a mutual friend for 05:08
as being from her birth certificate.

RR: AA   (Barbara Joan Streisand)
          Data Collectors: Frank Clifford; Edwin Steinbrecher

Notes:

PETER SUTCLIFFE

'The Yorkshire Ripper'; schizophrenic serial killer of 13 women;
violent assaults from 5/7/1975; arrested 2/1/1981; found guilty 5/1981

Sun ....

Moon ....

Ascendant ....

     Chart Ruler ....

Fire ....

Earth ....

Air ....

Water ....

Cardinal ....

Fixed ....

Mutable ....

Mutual Reception: Sign emphasis:

Unaspected: House emphasis:

Retrograde: Singletons/Duets:

Other chart points:

Equal Houses

ASPECTS & CONFIGURATIONS

THEMES & OTHER OBSERVATIONS

Placidus Houses

Born 2 June 1946, 20:30 GDT (-1)
Bingley, England (53n51, 1w50)
Source: Biography 'Somebody's Husband, Somebody's Son: The
Story of Peter Sutcliffe' by Gordon Burn (Heinemann, 1984),
p.13, '[Father] rang again at 10.30... he was told that he
was the father of a son who had been born about two hours
earlier... [he] decided he might as well stay the night.'
RR: B   (Peter William Sutcliffe)
Data Collectors: Sy Scholfield; Victoria Shaw

Notes:

MARGARET THATCHER

UK Prime Minister (4/5/1979–28/11/1990); MP from 8/10/59;
Tory leader from 11/2/1975; IRA Brighton bombing 12/10/1984

Sun ....

Moon ....

Ascendant ....

    Chart Ruler ....

Fire ....

Earth ....

Air ....

Water ....

Cardinal ....

Fixed ....

Mutable ....

Mutual Reception: Sign emphasis:

Unaspected: House emphasis:

Retrograde: Singletons/Duets:

Other chart points:

Equal Houses

Placidus Houses

ASPECTS & CONFIGURATIONS

THEMES & OTHER OBSERVATIONS

Born 13 October 1925, 09:00 GMT (+0)
Grantham, England (52n55, 0w39)

Source: From her private secretary to Charles Harvey.

RR: A

(Margaret Hilda Roberts)
Data Collector: Charles Harvey

Notes:

JUSTIN TIMBERLAKE

Singer-songwriter; member of pop band 'N Sync (1995–2002);
success from 8/1998; peak 3/2000; solo album 11/2002

Sun ....

Moon ....

Ascendant ....

      Chart Ruler ....

Fire ....

Earth ....

Air ....

Water ....

Cardinal ....

Fixed ....

Mutable ....

Mutual Reception: Sign emphasis:

Unaspected: House emphasis:

Retrograde: Singletons/Duets:

Other chart points:

ASPECTS & CONFIGURATIONS

THEMES & OTHER OBSERVATIONS

Equal Houses

Placidus Houses

Born 31 January 1981, 18:30 CST (+6)
Memphis, Tennessee, USA (35n09, 90w03)

Source: Birth certificate, copy on file.

RR: AA

(Justin Randall Timberlake)
Data Collector: Frank Clifford

Notes:

JOHN TRAVOLTA

Actor-singer; TV star from 9/9/1975; *Saturday Night Fever*
(14/12/1977), *Grease* (16/6/1978); resurgence in *Pulp Fiction* (5/1994)

Sun ....

Moon ....

Ascendant ....

       Chart Ruler ....

Fire ....

Earth ....

Air ....

Water ....

Cardinal ....

Fixed ....

Mutable ....

Mutual Reception: Sign emphasis:

Unaspected: House emphasis:

Retrograde: Singletons/Duets:

Other chart points:

Equal Houses

Placidus Houses

ASPECTS & CONFIGURATIONS

THEMES & OTHER OBSERVATIONS

Born 18 February 1954, 14:53 EST (+5)
Englewood, New Jersey, USA (40n54, 73w58)

Source: Birth certificate; same in 'Contemporary American
Horoscopes' and 'The Gauquelin Book of American Charts'.

RR: AA   (John Joseph Travolta)
Data Collectors: Eugene Moore;
Janice Mackay-Saunders; M. and F. Gauquelin

Notes:

DONALD TRUMP

Billionaire magnate; real estate developer; narrowly avoided
bankruptcy 5/1991; fronted TV's *The Apprentice* from 8/1/2004

Sun ....

Moon ....

Ascendant ....

     Chart Ruler ....

Fire ....

Earth ....

Air ....

Water ....

Cardinal ....

Fixed ....

Mutable ....

Mutual Reception: Sign emphasis:

Unaspected: House emphasis:

Retrograde: Singletons/Duets:

Other chart points:

Equal Houses

Placidus Houses

ASPECTS & CONFIGURATIONS

THEMES & OTHER OBSERVATIONS

Born 14 June 1946, 09:51 EDT (+4)
Queens, New York, USA (40n43, 73w52)

Source: From him, quoting his mother, to a trusted colleague
of Lois Rodden.

RR: A

(Donald John Trump)
Data Collector: Lois Rodden

Notes:

TED TURNER

Media mogul; founded CNN (prem. 1/6/1980) and TNT
(3/10/1988); married to Jane Fonda (qv) 21/12/1991–22/5/2001

Sun ....

Moon ....

Ascendant ....

    Chart Ruler ....

Fire ....

Earth ....

Air ....

Water ....

Cardinal ....

Fixed ....

Mutable ....

Mutual Reception: Sign emphasis:

Unaspected: House emphasis:

Retrograde: Singletons/Duets:

Other chart points:

Equal Houses

Placidus Houses

ASPECTS & CONFIGURATIONS

THEMES & OTHER OBSERVATIONS

Born 19 November 1938, 08:50 EST (+5)
Cincinnati, Ohio, USA (39n10, 84w27)

Source: Birth certificate, copy on file; same in 'Contemporary
American Horoscopes' and 'The Gauquelin Book of American
Charts'.

RR: AA

(Robert Edward Turner III)
Data Collector: Frank Clifford

Notes:

TINA TURNER

Singer; dynamic rock-soul 'lioness'; chart success with Ike
Turner from 10/1960; left Ike 7/1976; comeback from 12/1982

Sun ....

Moon ....

Ascendant ....

      Chart Ruler ....

Fire ....

Earth ....

Air ....

Water ....

Cardinal ....

Fixed ....

Mutable ....

Mutual Reception: Sign emphasis:

Unaspected: House emphasis:

Retrograde: Singletons/Duets:

Other chart points:

Equal Houses

ASPECTS & CONFIGURATIONS

THEMES & OTHER OBSERVATIONS

Placidus Houses

Born 26 November 1939, 22:10 CST (+6)
Nutbush, Tennessee, USA (35n42, 89w24)

Source: Note from birth registry, copy on file (born at
home). Same birth time from her to Marc Penfield.

RR: AA   (Martha Nell Bullock)
      Data Collectors: Frank Clifford; Marc Penfield

Notes:

QUEEN VICTORIA

British monarch; acceded on 20/6/1837 at 2:12 am; married
Prince Albert 10/2/1840; devastated by his death on 14/12/1861

Sun ....

Moon ....

Ascendant ....

    Chart Ruler ....

Fire ....

Earth ....

Air ....

Water ....

Cardinal ....

Fixed ....

Mutable ....

Mutual Reception: Sign emphasis:

Unaspected: House emphasis:

Retrograde: Singletons/Duets:

Other chart points:

Equal Houses

Placidus Houses

ASPECTS & CONFIGURATIONS

THEMES & OTHER OBSERVATIONS

Born 24 May 1819, 04:15 LMT (+0:00:32)
Kensington Palace, London, England (51n30, 0w08)

Source: Official royal bulletin as transcribed in 'The
Times', 26/5/1819, p.2.

RR: A   (Alexandrina Victoria Saxe-Coburg Hanover)
                Data Collector: Sy Scholfield

Notes:

NEALE DONALD WALSCH

Modern day spiritual messenger; author of the *Conversations with God* series (Book I pub. 1/10/1996); dialogue began 4/1992

Sun ....

Moon ....

Ascendant ....

    Chart Ruler ....

Fire ....

Earth ....

Air ....

Water ....

Cardinal ....

Fixed ....

Mutable ....

Mutual Reception:

Unaspected:

Retrograde:

Other chart points:

Sign emphasis:

House emphasis:

Singletons/Duets:

Equal Houses

Placidus Houses

ASPECTS & CONFIGURATIONS

THEMES & OTHER OBSERVATIONS

Born 10 September 1943, 04:19 CWT (+5)
Milwaukee, Wisconsin, USA (43n02, 87w54)

Source: Birth certificate.

RR: AA

(Neale Donald Walsch)
Data Collector: Stephen Przybylowski

Notes:

DIONNE WARWICK

Elegant, popular singer; fundraiser; met Bacharach & David
in 7/1961; ten years of hits from 1/1963; career resurgence 1979

Sun ....

Moon ....

Ascendant ....

    Chart Ruler ....

Fire ....

Earth ....

Air ....

Water ....

Cardinal ....

Fixed ....

Mutable ....

Mutual Reception: Sign emphasis:

Unaspected: House emphasis:

Retrograde: Singletons/Duets:

Other chart points:

Equal Houses

Placidus Houses

ASPECTS & CONFIGURATIONS

THEMES & OTHER OBSERVATIONS

Born 12 December 1940, 15:08 EST (+5)
Orange, New Jersey, USA (40n46, 74w14)

Source: Birth certificate quoted in 'Contemporary American
Horoscopes' and 'The Gauquelin Book of American Charts'.
Warwick gave 03:17 to Lynne Palmer.

(Marie Dionne Warrick)

RR: AA   Data Collectors: Janice Mackay-Saunders;
M. and F. Gauquelin; Lynne Palmer

Notes:

ORSON WELLES

Prodigious talent; director-actor-producer; infamous *The War of the Worlds* radio broadcast 30/10/1938; *Citizen Kane* 1/5/1941

Sun ....

Moon ....

Ascendant ....

     Chart Ruler ....

Fire ....

Earth ....

Air ....

Water ....

Cardinal ....

Fixed ....

Mutable ....

Mutual Reception: Sign emphasis:

Unaspected: House emphasis:

Retrograde: Singletons/Duets:

Other chart points:

Equal Houses

Placidus Houses

ASPECTS & CONFIGURATIONS

THEMES & OTHER OBSERVATIONS

Born 6 May 1915, 07:00 CST (+6)
Kenosha, Wisconsin, USA (42n35, 87w49)

Source: Birth certificate quoted in 'Contemporary American Horoscopes' and 'The Gauquelin Book of American Charts'.

RR: AA   (George Orson Welles)
Data Collectors: Janice Mackay-Saunders; M. and F. Gauquelin

Notes:

H.G. WELLS

Father of science fiction; socialist; *The Time Machine* (1894);
The Invisible Man (1897); *The War of the Worlds* (1898)

Sun ....

Moon ....

Ascendant ....

      Chart Ruler ....

Fire ....

Earth ....

Air ....

Water ....

Cardinal ....

Fixed ....

Mutable ....

Mutual Reception: Sign emphasis:

Unaspected: House emphasis:

Retrograde: Singletons/Duets:

Other chart points:

Equal Houses

Placidus Houses

ASPECTS & CONFIGURATIONS

THEMES & OTHER OBSERVATIONS

Born 21 September 1866, 16:30 GMT (+0)
Bromley, England (51n24, 0e02)

Source: His mother's diary quoted by the H.G. Wells Society
of Great Britain and in 'H. G. Wells: A Biography' by Norman
Ian MacKenzie & Jeanne MacKenzie (Simon and Schuster, 1973),
p.3.
RR: AA

                                (Herbert George Wells)
Data Collectors: Paul Wright; Sy Scholfield

Notes:

DR RUTH WESTHEIMER

Sex therapist and author; frank, enthusiastic TV and radio
personality from 9/1980; pioneer in 'sexual literacy'

Sun ....

Moon ....

Ascendant ....

     Chart Ruler ....

Fire ....

Earth ....

Air ....

Water ....

Cardinal ....

Fixed ....

Mutable ....

Mutual Reception: Sign emphasis:

Unaspected: House emphasis:

Retrograde: Singletons/Duets:

Other chart points:

ASPECTS & CONFIGURATIONS

THEMES & OTHER OBSERVATIONS

Equal Houses

Placidus Houses

Born 4 June 1928, 04:00 MET (-1)
Frankfurt am Main, Germany (50n07, 8e40)

Source: Westheimer to Evelyn Herbertz in 1985.

RR: A

(Karola Ruth Siegel)
Data Collector: Evelyn Herbertz

Notes:

OSCAR WILDE

Playwright, poet, aesthete, social celebrity, wit; accusation of
sodomy on 18/2/1895 led to libel trial (4/1895) and gaol (5/1895)

Sun ....

Moon ....

Ascendant ....

    Chart Ruler ....

Fire ....

Earth ....

Air ....

Water ....

Cardinal ....

Fixed ....

Mutable ....

Mutual Reception: Sign emphasis:

Unaspected: House emphasis:

Retrograde: Singletons/Duets:

Other chart points:

Equal Houses

Placidus Houses

ASPECTS & CONFIGURATIONS

THEMES & OTHER OBSERVATIONS

Born 16 October 1854, 03:00 LMT (+0:25:00)
Dublin, Ireland (53n20, 6w15)

Source: Baptismal certificate quoted by Cyril Fagan. (Lover
'Bosie', Lord Alfred Douglas, was born 22 October 1870,
19:50 GMT (+0), Ham Hill, Worcester, England (52n10, 2w15).
From him, 'Mother said 7.30 to 8pm, closer to 8.')
RR: AA   (Oscar Fingal O'Flahertie Wills Wilde)
     Data Collector: Cyril Fagan

Notes:

TENNESSEE WILLIAMS

Celebrated playwright; *A Streetcar Named Desire* (prem.
3/12/1947); *Cat on a Hot Tin Roof* (24/3/1955); alcoholic, depressive

Sun ....

Moon ....

Ascendant ....

      Chart Ruler ....

Fire ....

Earth ....

Air ....

Water ....

Cardinal ....

Fixed ....

Mutable ....

Mutual Reception: Sign emphasis:

Unaspected: House emphasis:

Retrograde: Singletons/Duets:

Other chart points:

Equal Houses

Placidus Houses

ASPECTS & CONFIGURATIONS

THEMES & OTHER OBSERVATIONS

Born 26 March 1911, 02:30 CST (+6)
Columbus, Mississippi, USA (33n30, 88w26)

Source: From him to Emma Cates. A time of 02:25 was given by
Williams to Bob Prince.

RR: A   (Thomas Lanier Williams III)
                           Data Collector: Gene Lockhart

Notes:

VENUS WILLIAMS

Powerful tennis World #1 from 25/2/2002, then eclipsed by
sister Serena; Olympic gold (9/2000); pro from 31/10/1994

Sun ....

Moon ....

Ascendant ....

      Chart Ruler ....

Fire ....

Earth ....

Air ....

Water ....

Cardinal ....

Fixed ....

Mutable ....

Mutual Reception: Sign emphasis:

Unaspected: House emphasis:

Retrograde: Singletons/Duets:

Other chart points:

Equal Houses

Placidus Houses

ASPECTS & CONFIGURATIONS

THEMES & OTHER OBSERVATIONS

Born 17 June 1980, 14:12 PDT (+7)
Lynwood, California, USA (33n56, 118w13)

Source: Birth certificate, copy on file. (Her sister Serena
Jameka Williams was born 26 September 1981, 20:28 EDT (+4),
Saginaw, Michigan, USA (43n25, 83w57). Birth certificate from
the Hall of Records, as quoted by Shelley Ackerman.)
RR: AA   (Venus Ebony Starr Williams)
                   Data Collector: Frank Clifford

Notes:

AMY WINEHOUSE

Singer-songwriter; debut album *Frank* (rel. 10/2003); follow-up *Back to Black* (10/2006); addiction battles and turmoil

Sun ....

Moon ....

Ascendant ....

      Chart Ruler ....

Fire ....

Earth ....

Air ....

Water ....

Cardinal ....

Fixed ....

Mutable ....

Mutual Reception: Sign emphasis:

Unaspected: House emphasis:

Retrograde: Singletons/Duets:

Other chart points:

Equal Houses

Placidus Houses

ASPECTS & CONFIGURATIONS

THEMES & OTHER OBSERVATIONS

Born 14 September 1983, 22:25 GDT (-1)
Enfield, London, England (51n40, 0w05)

Source: From Winehouse's mother to a mutual friend of astrologer Margaret Zelinski.

RR: A

(Amy Jade Winehouse)
Data Collector: Margaret Zelinski

Notes:

TIGER WOODS

World-class, record-breaking golfer; world's highest earning
sportsman; turned pro 8/1996; dominated 6/1999–2002, 2005–7

Sun ....

Moon ....

Ascendant ....

     Chart Ruler ....

Fire ....

Earth ....

Air ....

Water ....

Cardinal ....

Fixed ....

Mutable ....

Mutual Reception: Sign emphasis:

Unaspected: House emphasis:

Retrograde: Singletons/Duets:

Other chart points:

Equal Houses

Placidus Houses

ASPECTS & CONFIGURATIONS

THEMES & OTHER OBSERVATIONS

Born 30 December 1975, 22:50 PST (+8)
Long Beach, California, USA (33n46, 118w11)

Source: Birth certificate.

RR: AA

(Eldrick Tont Woods)
Data Collector: Lois Rodden

Notes:

_____

Sun ....

Moon ....

Ascendant ....

      Chart Ruler ....

Fire ....

Earth ....

Air ....

Water ....

Cardinal ....

Fixed ....

Mutable ....

Equal Houses

Mutual Reception: Sign emphasis:

Unaspected: House emphasis:

Retrograde: Singletons/Duets:

Other chart points:

Placidus Houses

ASPECTS & CONFIGURATIONS

THEMES & OTHER OBSERVATIONS

Notes:

Sun ....

Moon ....

Ascendant ....

     Chart Ruler ....

Fire ....

Earth ....

Air ....

Water ....

Cardinal ....

Fixed ....

Mutable ....

Mutual Reception: Sign emphasis:

Unaspected: House emphasis:

Retrograde: Singletons/Duets:

Other chart points:

Equal Houses

10 9 8
11 12 7
1 6
2 5
3 4

ASPECTS & CONFIGURATIONS

THEMES & OTHER OBSERVATIONS

Placidus Houses

10 9 8
11 12 7
1 6
2 5
3 4

Notes:

Sun ....

Moon ....

Ascendant ....

      Chart Ruler ....

Fire ....

Earth ....

Air ....

Water ....

Cardinal ....

Fixed ....

Mutable ....

Mutual Reception: Sign emphasis:

Unaspected: House emphasis:

Retrograde: Singletons/Duets:

Other chart points:

Equal Houses

ASPECTS & CONFIGURATIONS

THEMES & OTHER OBSERVATIONS

Placidus Houses

Notes:

CPSIA information can be obtained
at www.ICGtesting.com
Printed in the USA
BVOW07s2348280417
482604BV00003B/9/P